Lytham St
Transport

Harry Postlethwaite

© 2009 Venture Publications Ltd

ISBN 978 1905 304 288

Contents

Introduction

The Borough of Lytham St Annes was formed in November 1922 by the amalgamation of the Urban District of St Annes on the Sea and the Urban District of Lytham. On formation it took control of the St Annes on the Sea Council Tramways. As part of local government reorganisation the Borough was extended as from 1st April 1974 to include the Kirkham Urban District Council and Fylde Rural District Council. Like many other historic towns caught up in this reorganisation the enlarged borough received a somewhat nondescript name, in this case 'The Borough of Fylde', which is inaccurate to say the least, as the Borough does not cover the whole of the area known for many years as 'The Fylde'. However, over thirty years later the name has not caught on, other than for local government legalities, and to locals and the many visitors which it receives, it will always be Lytham St Annes.

The change in name of the Borough brought about a change in name for the Transport Department, a name which was to be further changed under the 1985 Transport Act and again when the undertaking was sold to its management. As a result of these changes there is a quite complex history to what has always been a relatively small undertaking.

Producing this latest in my series on Lancashire operators has been both pleasurable and revealing giving me a greater insight into what happened within a few miles of my present home long before it was built or we moved here.

The opportunity to turn the clock back through old photographs, timetables and publicity material is one I hope you will enjoy sharing with me.

Harry Postlethwaite
Little Bispham
May 2009

Opposite: What was probably a Sunday School outing makes good use of two of the electric trams – note the different construction with the open sides on the nearer car.

Below: The tide is out, and so is the sun. A small selection of 1930s motor cars keep company with the Guy runabout bus, seen right. *(STA/JNC both)*

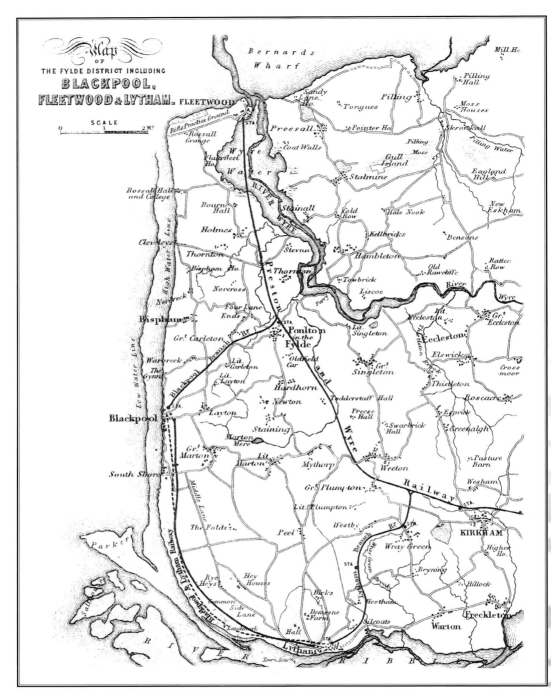

This map, dating from c189x, neatly shows the Fylde area described in the following pages. Lytham will be seen in the centre at the very bottom, with St Annes, not marked, being further to the west. The dotted line shows the route of the tramway along Clifton Drive to Blackpool. Preston, mentioned in Chapter 2 in relation to a proposal to extend the tramway, is 12 miles upstream of the River Ribble whose estuary forms the bottom of the map. (STA/JNC)

1 – *Early Days of Transport in the Area*

The story starts in 1880 when a scheme was proposed for the operation of a horse drawn tramway system between Blackpool, St Annes and Lytham, but as the area was sparsely populated and as the proposed route was parallel to the railway, the scheme came to nought and no further action took place until 24th August 1893, the date of the incorporation of the Blackpool, St Annes and Lytham Tramways Company. This company received Parliamentary sanction to take over the powers granted in 1880 and was authorised to construct and operate a tramway from Rigby Road, Blackpool via Lytham Road, Clifton Drive and St Annes to Clifton Square, Lytham. The powers to construct the section within Blackpool were not to be exercised unless Blackpool Corporation failed to construct the section within 12 months under their own powers. If Blackpool did build the section within their Borough, they were required to lease it to the Company for a period of 21 years from the date of opening.

Blackpool Corporation did build their section and on 26th September 1895 commenced a tramway service operating on the 'conduit' principle from the Manchester Hotel along Lytham Road to Station Road which connected with a horse drawn shuttle service operating between Station Road and Squires Gate, this being necessary because the Company had not completed their line. Furthermore, the time for the completion of the works, two years from the date of the Act, had passed and this meant that a further application had to be made to Parliament to revive the Company's powers and to extend the date for completion of the construction.

The revived powers reached the Statute Book as the Blackpool, St Annes and Lytham Tramways Act 1896 and received Royal Assent on 20th July 1897. The period for completion of the works was extended until 12 months from the date of the Act. It confirmed the Agreement with Blackpool and empowered the Company to acquire and operate omnibuses in conjunction with their tramway in St Annes and Lytham.

The flywheel side of one of the gas trams. Opening the two doors in the side panels allowed the driver to crank the engine into life. Two gas storage cylinders can be seen slung below the underframe and cooling pipes are visible below the upper deck decency panels. The driver had a conventional tram handbrake and a lever to operate the clutch which then engaged the driveshaft. Gas leaks and oil fumes created a most unpleasant environment in the lower deck. *(JNC)*

In the meantime, the tramway had already opened between Station Road and St Annes on 11th July 1896 with the extension to Lytham opening on 21st February 1897. The initial rolling stock comprised four cars built by Ashbury Railway Carriage and Iron Company of Manchester in 1896 and driven by water cooled horizontally opposed twin cylinder 15hp Otto gas engines built in Germany. The engine was situated under the seats on one side of the lower deck with a flywheel situated between the engine and the outside panelling of the tramcar. A hinged opening was provided for access. The town gas was stored at a pressure of 120psi (8bar) in three cylinders, one under the lower saloon seats and two mounted transversely under the car at each end. The cars seated 40, 16 on the lower deck and 24 on the upper deck and in view of the low power output of the engine there were times when passengers had to get out and push on the railway bridges at Stoney Hill and South Shore.

A further 16 gas trams were built in 1897 by Lancashire Carriage and Wagon Company, Lancaster and were larger than the original four seating 52 passengers with 30 on the upper deck and 22 in the lower deck. Surprisingly, these had the same engines as the smaller cars but better gearing gave them a higher maximum speed of 12mph as opposed to the 9mph limit of the others.

Depots were established at the junction of Lytham Road and Squires Gate Lane and also at Henry Street, Lytham. The Squires Gate Lane depot was opened on 11th July 1896 and the Henry Street depot, converted from a roller skating rink and situated on the north side of Henry Street, Lytham, on 21st February 1897. The Squires Gate Lane depot was originally a small tram car shed and stables which was rebuilt as an eight track dead-ended tram depot for electric overhead operation in June 1903. In 1910 all the roads were extended into a works section at the rear of the building and a four track dead-ended extension was added on the east side in March 1924. The depot was used to accommodate omnibuses from 6th August 1923.

The Company did not operate the tramway but leased it for operational purposes to the British Gas Traction Company Limited who agreed to operate the system at a rate of 4.5d per car mile run with a minimum of 163,000 miles per annum. The cost per mile included the wages of the driver but the conductor was employed by the Tramway Company. At first the service was infrequent with two cars in traffic and providing a 40 minutes service between St Annes and Blackpool South Shore. In the following year the number of cars was increased to 20. The cars operated on ordinary town gas which was compressed at a charging station at Squires Gate corner and another at Cambridge Road, Ansdell and carried in cylinders on the cars. Recharging took place by means of a flexible hose, a process which took about two minutes. The gas engines could be run on one or two cylinders, according to requirements, with a choice of two gear trains selected through a clutch. In the winter of 1896/7 the total number of passengers carried was 78,000 but this rose to 200,000 in the summer of 1897 and to 500,000 the following summer. The number of trams used in winter was six but this increased to 14 in summer to provide a 10 minutes service.

On 15th October 1898 a new limited company was registered under the name of the Blackpool,

The water cooling pipes increased the height of the cars and the original cowcatcher lifeguard did little to enhance the appearance. Number 16 is from the second, larger batch. *(STA/JNC)*

St Annes and Lytham Tramways Company Limited and took over the assets of the system including the cars and the equipment belonging to the British Gas Traction Company Limited. Blackpool Corporation agreed under certain conditions to assign the lease to the new Company. The Statutory Company was wound up under an order of the Court of the Chancery of the County Palatine of Lancaster dated 21st November 1898. The British Gas Traction Company Limited encountered financial difficulties and a winding up order was made against it in early autumn 1899 at which time it agreed to surrender its lease. The limited company had taken over operation of the tramways on 8th August 1899.

The gas trams were unsatisfactory and in April 1900 a total of 17 secondhand horse drawn trams were purchased from Bolton Corporation at a cost of £500. These horse trams were taken out of service in 1901 when operation remained entirely with the gas trams.

In August 1900 an Act had been passed authorising the conversion of the system to electric operation using an overhead system, Blackpool Corporation having already abandoned the use of the conduit system in 1898. Royal Assent was granted on 8th August 1900 and included the authority to construct a new line to serve Lytham Hospital and confirmed the agreement to assign the Blackpool lease to the new company. Reconstruction began in December 1902 with Blackpool Corporation converting the section within their boundary.

There was a further change of ownership in early, 1901 when the company was sold to the Electric Tramways Construction and Maintenance Company Limited for the sum of £111,000. Another company, Blackpool Electric Tramways (South) Limited was formed and applied for an Order to extend the Lytham line to Preston with the intention being that, after completion of the electrification, it would acquire the Blackpool to Lytham section and operate the whole system as one. The Order was, however, refused.

On 27th February 1903, the Squires Gate depot was demolished in a gale and the cars inside were buried beneath the debris. A total of 13 cars were damaged and it is presumed that the other 7 cars were in Lytham depot. This settled the fate of the gas cars but some were salvaged and saw further service at Trafford Park Estates

The Gas Tram Company seems to have been designed to make money only for the promoters; baling it out saddled the undertaking with sufficient debt to make sure that Lytham's trams never made a penny for the shareholders or the Council. Small wonder the local paper, aware of the background scenario, thought this proposal had some merit. See also the extracts overleaf. *(STA/JNC)*

"**THE MANCHESTER CHRONICLE**" (March 28th, 1901), says :—

IT is good news to Blackpool to learn that the statement to the effect that the Lytham and St. Annes Tramway Company's undertaking has been acquired by a Syndicate, who are about to seek powers to construct a Tramway from Preston to Blackpool, where it will join the system now running to Blackpool, turns out to be true. It is claimed for the Blackpool Corporation Electric that they were the first, not only in England, but in the world; their success is almost too well known to need comment. Hundreds of visitors to the sea coast pleasure resorts have made good use of the cars at their disposal, and the profits have been high.

The new undertaking will be a large one, and the capital of the new Company will be about £350,000. The

line is to be doubled without delay,

and will be equipped with all the latest improvements. The track is to be extended to Preston, to which town the Blackpool, St. Annes, and Lytham Trams already travel nearly halfway. The consummation of this scheme will be of immense benefit to Preston; in fact, the whole district within the influence of the new extension will be enriched. One effect of the new line to Preston will be that many journeying to Blackpool and its sister resorts will be

able to alight at Preston

and reach their destinations by the Electric Cars.

The present Blackpool-Lytham line has about a mile further to construct. This will be finished and then the road will go on to Freckleton, and thence, as a light railway to Preston. It is expected that the whole country side will be opened up *en route*. The phenominal growth of Blackpool, and the general prosperity of Lancashire are happy auguries for the success of the new scheme.

———:———

From "THE BLACKPOOL TIMES," March 27th, 1901.

Blackpool to Preston by Tram.

Purchase of the Blackpool-Lytham Tramway. — More Extensions.

"THE BLACKPOOL TIMES" says :—

IN these dull days one matter alone seems to carry with it success. Whatever pays or does not pay, a Tramway pays when it has half a success.

The success of the Blackpool and Fleetwood System is too well known to need comment. The shares are now at a full £4 premium, and the Blackpool Corporation Trams have been a great success, and have contributed materially to the relief of rates.

We are given to und...

...adequate idea of how Blackpool appears when the Tramway routes are literally black with ...ded as rapidly as they can run, following on incessantly without respect to Time Tables.

...HE BLACKPOOL, ST. ANNES AND ...LYTHAM TRAMWAYS.

...he long looked for and inevitable ...last! The line has been pur-...east so the secretary's circular ...ore popular news to Blackpool ...o be difficult to conceive.

...of thousands of Tramway ...ers have longed for this con-...

...g welcome intelligence is that ...ill be doubled without delay. It ...uipped with all that the latest ...lectrical plant can do. The ...o be a revelation of luxury and ...and, still greater news—the ...e continued to Preston.

... PRESTON LINE.

...ckpool, St. Annes and Lytham ...eady travel nearly half way ...at town.

...this mean? A change for ...connected to Preston by

...00,000 population, or perhaps ...noo, are brought nearer by ...nd swift Electric cars run ...inutes.

the character of the whole town become... affected. There will be more continuous... more steady, progress.

Property in the town will be affected both here and all along the route. Wha... will it do for Preston? Preston will soon begin to live at the seaside. A few minutes' run by tram, and the beautiful meadows of Freckleton and the shore of the Ribble will be reached. Suc... places as Freckleton, Lytham, and th... other places along the route will becom... increasingly important.

COMPARE THE FLEETWOOD LINE

with such a comparatively insignificant tow... as the terminus, and nothing on the way, wit... the new Tramway, having no less a town tha...

Preston, with its factories, docks, an... tens of thousands of operatives an... workpeople at one end, and no less ... town than Blackpool at the othe...

THE BLOCK AT PRESTON.

The Lancashire millions com... this way to Blackpool,

that is, via Preston. What more natural tha... that after being done to death in a cramp... up, dusty and sultry railway carriage for sever...

"THE BLACKPOOL HERALD" (March 29th, 1901), says :—

THE converting of the Lytham and St. Annes Tramway from the gas traction system to the Electrical Overhead System is now assured. By almost insensible stages, the undertaking has passed under a new control. Instead of proceeding by the usual course of purchasing the company and its undertaking from its owners, the Electrical Syndicate has bought up something like three-fourths of the share capital at market prices, and so acquired control. The Company acquired powers last year to convert their line to an Electrical System by a special Act of Parliament, and this will enable the Syndicate to proceed with the work at once. It is the sanguine estimate of the promoters that

Electrically driven Cars will be running between Blackpool and Lytham next Easter.

The Liverpool syndicate were very positive and thereby attracted good coverage in the local press. The general feeling was that anything had to be better than the smelly, noisy, vibrating gas trams. Looking at the terrain between Lytham and Blackpool the obvious lack of passenger potential was plain to see. And onwards to Preston? Flights of fancy perhaps come no bigger than this scheme. *(STA/JNC)*

Limited, Manchester and in Neath, South Wales, in this latter case being initially operated by the Provincial Gas Traction Company until 1916 when the Corporation took over. The gas trams survived at Neath until 1920.

The line reopened with electric traction with power being switched on during the night of 20th May 1903 with the first trial run being made the following morning. Mr Alexander F Trotter inspected the electrical equipment of the line on behalf of the Board of Trade on 27th May 1903 and on Thursday 28th May, Major Druitt inspected and accepted the line subject to certain stipulated speed limits being imposed. Only ten trams were available for the first public service on Saturday 30th May with the balance of twenty due to be delivered in time for the summer season. Recognising that these ten would be unable to cope arrangements were made to hire some cars from neighbouring Blackpool.

Blackpool, St. Annes and Lytham Tramways Company Limited

Offices:
300, Lytham Road, South Shore, Blackpool.

Winter Arrangements, 1905-6.

The Company herewith enclose their **Winter Time Table** for the use of residents on the route. All the pages are printed separately on cards for local use, and may be had on application at the Offices of the Company, or n the Local Agents at St. Annes and Lytham. It will seen that provision is made for a service of cars on Sunday mornings. On receiving notice of any concert, private party, or other entertainment, the Company will provide late evening services.

All cars will run through to Central Station, except some late cars specially indicated in the Time Table.

A considerable Revision of Fares has been made to meet the requirements of local traffic, including the following, viz.:—

The Penny Fare between South Shore and Squires Gate is extended to Golf House.

A Single Penny Town Stage has been arranged through St. Annes, viz., between Beach Road and Lightburne Avenue.

The route followed the line of the gas and horse trams along the sand dunes from Blackpool to St Annes, then via Clifton Drive South to Ansdell and along Church Road to Lytham Square and past the old gas tram depot where it turned south towards the shore, terminating in Dicconson Terrace opposite the pier. In September 1903 a one mile extension was opened along Clifton Street and Warton Street to terminate at the Lytham Hospital.

A new depot was built on the south side of Squires Gate Lane and opened in June 1904. It survived until the end of operations in 1999. Workshops at the rear were added in 1910 and the office block in 1911. The Henry Street depot was closed on 26th February 1903 and was not converted for electric traction but it was used during the winter of 1903/4 to store cars which were now not required for service. When the company was sold to the local authority, it was described as 'the picture pavilion known as the Hippodrome'. The building was demolished in 1986.

In a reversal on the earlier situation Blackpool now stored cars, rather than hiring them; Lytham cars were accommodated at Blackpool's Marton depot and in the Fleetwood Company's depots at Bispham and Copse Road, Fleetwood. Later, the depot was leased as a cinema.

The electric cars terminated at Station Road, Blackpool until the summer of 1905 when, after protracted negotiations with Blackpool Corporation, agreement was reached for the company's cars to operate to Central Station via Waterloo Road and Central Drive. In the summer season, cars also operated to the Manchester Hotel via Lytham Road and to Victoria Pier (now South Pier) via Station Road. In the same year a further application was made for powers to extend the line to Preston but this was rejected. However, authority was granted for an unorthodox tramway across the Ribble estuary between Lytham and Southport. The intention was that cars should cross the river on a type of transporter bridge but the powers lapsed with the passage of time and no further action was taken. The journeys to Victoria Pier ceased in March 1912 and when the Lytham Road lease was due to expire in 1917 Blackpool declined to renew it but, under an Agreement dated 10th February 1917, granted running powers so that company cars continued to operate as before but Blackpool introduced their own service along Lytham Road.

The Tramway and Light Railway Congress took place in Blackpool in 1913 and delegates were able to sample the Lytham open-top toastrack trams shown overleaf. In August that same year the company purchased its first motor vehicle, a 34hp Daimler painted red, and used it on excursions to Morecambe, Southport and the Lake District.

Blackpool, St. Annes and Lytham Tramways.

NEW DOUBLE-DECK OPEN CARS.

[Reprint from the "St. Annes Express."]

The Blackpool, St. Annes and Lytham Electric Tramways Co. have shown commendable enterprise and consideration for their holiday patrons by providing a number of open cars for the summer traffic. Ten cars, each capable of seating 68 passengers (inside and out), have been ordered from the Brush Electrical Engineering Co. The cars are handsome in design and are built on a new principle, known as the "radical truck," which gives a certain amount of free play in the axle box. It enables the wheel base to be increased from six feet to nine feet, thereby giving a very steady motion to the car and enabling it to get round a sharp curve with ease. Thus the passenger will secure the greatest amount of comfort. In windy or wet weather a strong canvas waterproof screen will cover the car on the weather side. It is only intended to use these cars in fine weather during the summer time. They are, essentially, cars for holiday traffic, being constructed in such a manner as to give ample room and the greatest comfort in the seating accommodation.

The first 30 electric cars were conventional four wheel open-toppers built by the British Electric Car Company. Perhaps someone from the undertaking had been to the Isle of Man and seen the Douglas Head cars when they were ready to order the next ten from Brush in a move which was inspired and resulted in ten of the first batch later being rebuilt by Brush to match their own product. They would become Lytham's most iconic and best-loved tramcars. *(STA/JNC)*

The Lytham cars had a variety of operating territory which was much more interesting than big neighbour Blackpool. From the genteel streets of their home town across the prairie-like Clifton Drive, through Blackpool's quieter suburbs and eventually into the brash heart of the town. The wild nature of the stretch between the dunes is well captured in these two lower photographs and behind car 26, rebuilt as a works car, grinder-cum-sand sweeper, men can be seen shovelling sand off the tracks. But to really see what it could be like after a good westerly blow turn to page 21. *(STA/JNC)*

It was not used on local services. The outbreak of the first World War prevented the extension of the excursions and the chassis was requisitioned by the War Office in September 1914 for use at Aldershot. The body remained with the company.

The all-male workforce were paraded for this photograph outside the depot in 1912, little dreaming that within two years they would be on a very different sort of parade ground. Some three years later women have moved into the workshops and the lathes are busy turning shell cases instead of armatures. Scenes like this were common throughout tramway and railway workshops in Britain. Paradoxically, Lytham were not alone in finding this work was considerably more profitable than running trams! *(STA/JNC)*

2 – St Annes on the Sea Urban District Council

Under the Tramways Act 1870, local authorities became entitled to purchase the portion of the undertaking within their district. St Annes on the Sea Urban District Council accordingly opened negotiations with the company in 1919 and an Agreement was completed on 3rd November 1919 which provided for the sale of the company's assets, except for investments and one plot of land, to the District Council. Parliamentary sanction was obtained as the St Annes on the Sea Urban District Council Act 1920 which received Royal Assent on 4th August 1920. This Act confirmed the Purchase Agreement, empowered the District Council to work the tramways and to provide and operate omnibuses in their District and within Lytham Urban District. On 28th October 1920 the tramway, including the Squires Gate depot, was purchased for £144,936 by St Annes Urban District Council. The transaction was financed by a loan of £132,279 4s 8d repayable over 30 years. Lytham had considered buying that part of the tramway which lay within its boundaries but a Bill to promote this was rejected by the House of Lords Standing Orders Committee. Lytham Council was to receive 25% of the profits earned by the tramways within their District and operation by St Annes commenced on 1st December 1920 operating as 'St Annes on the Sea Council Tramways'.

The Council appointed as its General Manager Mr Harry W Laing who had been Manager of the Cambridge Motor Omnibus Company since leaving the Paisley District Tramways Company.

The ceremony to mark the purchase of the tramway by St Annes Council was accorded its rightful place in history when the local photographer recorded the handing over of the cheque. Cllr CF Critchley, Mayor of St Annes and Chairman of the Transport Committee, makes the presentation to G Nicholson, his counterpart as Chairman of the Blackpool and Lytham Tramway Co, on 28th October 1920. Although the move was arguably both sensible and necessary it would be no money-spinner for Lytham. *(STA/JNC)*

ST ANNES COUNCIL TRAMWAYS.
C.F. Critchley Esq~ Chairman of Council~ handing over CHEQUES value £144,936:5:5~ to~ G. Nicholson Esq Chairman of BLACKPOOL ST ANNES & LYTHAM TRAMWAY Co LTD, in completion of PURCHASE of COMPANYS UNDERTAKING~ October 28th 1920~

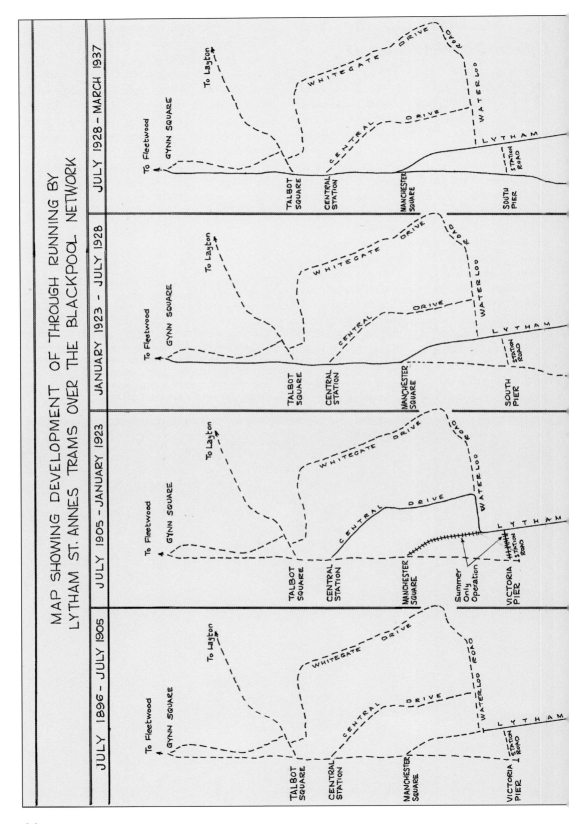

MAP SHOWING DEVELOPMENT OF THROUGH RUNNING BY
LYTHAM ST. ANNES TRAMS OVER THE BLACKPOOL NETWORK

JULY 1896 – JULY 1905

JULY 1905 – JANUARY 1923

JANUARY 1923 – JULY 1928

JULY 1928 – MARCH 1937

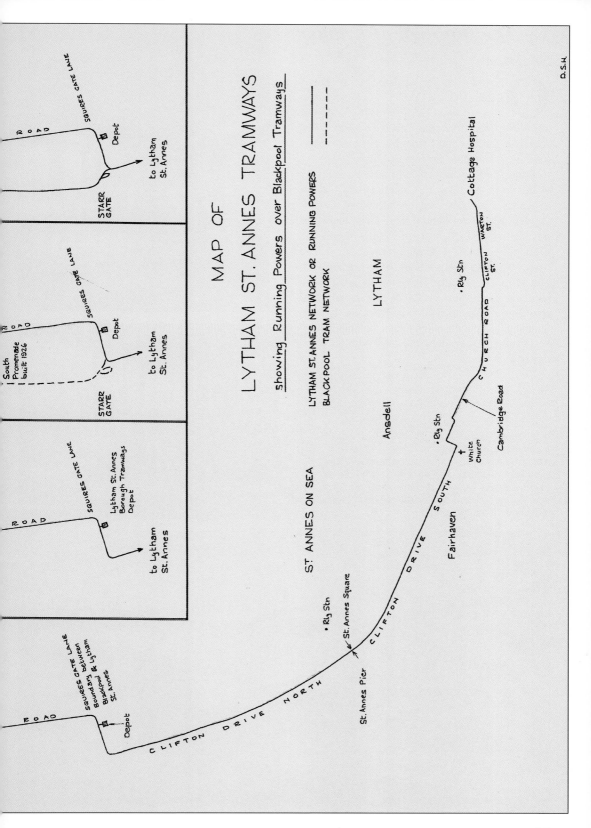

MAP OF
LYTHAM ST. ANNES TRAMWAYS

Showing Running Powers over Blackpool Tramways

LYTHAM ST. ANNES NETWORK OR RUNNING POWERS ————
BLACKPOOL TRAM NETWORK - - - - - - -

ROAD
SQUIRES GATE LANE
Lytham St. Annes
Borough Tramways
Depot
to Lytham
St. Annes

ROAD
South
Promenade
built 1926
SQUIRES GATE LANE
STARR
GATE
Depot
to Lytham
St. Annes

ROAD
SQUIRES GATE LANE
STARR
GATE
Depot
to Lytham
St. Annes

ROAD
SQUIRES GATE LANE
Boundary between
Blackpool & Lytham
St. Annes
Depot

CLIFTON DRIVE NORTH
St. Annes Pier
• Rly Stn
St. Annes Square

ST. ANNES ON SEA

CLIFTON DRIVE SOUTH

Fairhaven
• Rly Stn
White Church

Ansdell

LYTHAM

Cambridge Road

CHURCH ROAD
• Rly Stn
CLIFTON
ST.
WARTON
ST.
Cottage Hospital

D.S.H.

15

3 – The Borough of Lytham St Annes

Operation of the system by St Annes Urban District Council was destined to be short-lived because, with effect from 9th November 1922, the Urban Districts of St Annes on the Sea and Lytham were combined to form the Borough of Lytham St Annes.

From 22nd January 1923, prior to the relaying of the worn-out track in Central Drive, Lytham St Annes cars ceased to operate along Central Drive to Blackpool Central Station and thereafter travelled along Lytham Road and the Promenade to Talbot Square. Operating powers to extend further north to Gynn Square were granted with effect from 23rd July 1926 and in addition to reducing congestion in Talbot Square provided connection at Gynn Square between the Lytham St Annes and the Fleetwood cars, facilitating an 18 mile journey along the coast with only one change of car.

The arrival of ten balcony top-covered trams, numbered 41-50, in 1924 marked the last purchase of new rolling stock for the tramway. In a bold move they were fitted with upholstered 2+1 seating in the lower deck, but those who chose to ride upstairs would find nothing had changed and the hard and uncomfortable wooden seats remained. *(STA/JNC)*

Mayor CF Critchley tries the controls of the first of the balcony top-covered trams in 1925 which, as seen opposite, had transverse upholstered seats in the lower saloon. The by-now change to a lighter shade of blue and in the style of numerals is also evident in this close-up view. The familiar and awkward reversed staircase is still prominent, baulking the driver's nearside vision. It was destined to be the last tram to run in Lytham. *(STA)*

LYTHAM TRAMS

GO TO LYTHAM

BY ELECTRIC CAR

Back in Lytham in 1924 the depot had been extended to accommodate the increased fleet comprising new tramcars numbers 41-50, the first covered top examples to be operated.

The operation of local bus services within the Borough commenced in September 1923 when two 20-seat Guys entered service on a 'back street' route between St Annes and Lytham; a further four similar vehicles were purchased the same year followed by three more in 1924. The next bus was a small-wheeled diminutive Guy runabout, R1 in the fleet numbering system, designed to carry sightseers at slow speeds and to be able to pick up at will, subject to the regulations.

In response to this steady growth a document entitled *'Bye Laws and Regulations relating to*

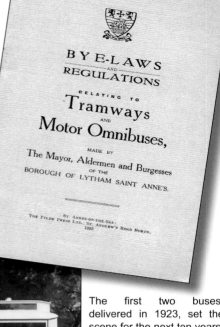

BYE-LAWS
AND
REGULATIONS

RELATING TO

Tramways
AND
Motor Omnibuses,

MADE BY

The Mayor, Aldermen and Burgesses
OF THE
BOROUGH OF LYTHAM SAINT ANNE'S.

ST ANNES-ON-THE-SEA:
THE FYLDE PRESS LTD., ST. ANDREW'S ROAD NORTH.
1925

The first two buses, delivered in 1923, set the scene for the next ten years, for, with only one exception, all subsequent purchases were also of Guy chassis. Numbers 1-7 were all Guy B models bodied by Blackburn Aeroplane & Motor Co of Olympia, Leeds. Number 1 is seen at the builders, and soon after entering service. *(STA/JNC)*

Tramways and Motor Omnibuses' made by the Mayor, Aldermen and Burgesses of the Borough of Lytham St Annes was published in 1925.

It was signed by the Mayor, CF Critchley, and the Town Clerk, T Bradley, on 28th September 1925 and countersigned by Cyril Hurcombe, Principal Assistant Secretary to the Ministry of Transport on 29th December 1925.

The *Bye Laws and Regulations* came into operation on 1st January 1926 and in that year three more of the small Guy buses arrived and a further service was commenced from Lytham Square to Meadow Lane, on the Preston Road; as this duplicated the tram service between the Square and the Hospital, the latter service to the Hospital was withdrawn from 23rd July 1926. There would be a pause now as the economic climate deteriorated, and no more buses would join the fleet for five years.

On 6th July 1928 following the extension of the Blackpool Tramways along the new South Promenade, a junction was provided at Starr Gate at the western end of Squires Gate Lane and alternate Lytham cars were diverted over this route during the summer months.

In 1929, with financial matters showing no improvement, the Council decided to part company with its Manager. Harry Laing, who had been in post since 1920, was asked to resign but elected instead to retire. Laing had been Traffic Superintendent at the Paisley District Tramways Company until 1905, then with Cambridge Motor Omnibus Company until joining Lytham. He thus had apparently had little or no experience of

Small wheels and consequent slow speeds made for an ideal sightseeing vehicle – provided you had short legs! Fleet number R1 remained as one of a fleet of one but appears in many photographs and picture postcards of the town, often at the pier terminus. The unusual bodywork was built by chassis maker Guy of Wolverhampton. *(STA/JNC)*

electric tramway operation.

The purchase of the expensive Pullman cars which, it would appear, may not have really been needed, at a time of financial stringency, may also have hastened his demise.

John Cameron Fairchild was then appointed to the combined post of Borough Electrical Engineer and Manager. His tenure would last until November 1946 when he would be succeeded by his deputy, W Ashton, who had joined the Lytham Company way back in 1910 as a junior.

With Fairchild's installation, the Tramways Department was now renamed Transport Department, reflecting the growing importance of the 12 (13 with the runabout) buses in the fleet, and also keeping in line with fashionable trends in the industry!

It was around this time that the railway companies were seeking to get a foothold into the growing bus industry and in January 1931 an offer was received – and rejected – from the London Midland and Scottish Railway Company for the takeover of the undertaking. Later in the same year there were talks – also abortive – with Ribble Motor Services about co-ordination.

In 1935 Lytham began supporting local bus manufacturers Leyland and Burlingham with the purchase of these two Cubs. *(STA/JNC)*

When the next buses came in that same year they included the first pair of full-sized – 31-seat – examples, and a further three small 20-seaters, all Guys and all second-hand.

Two years later, in 1933, further additions to the fleet arrived at Squires Gate depot, but this time a very mixed bag indeed. Pride of place, and marking a major change in policy, came two new Leyland Cubs, numbered 2 and 8, with 20-seat bodywork by local builder HV Burlingham of Blackpool. Eight second-hand Guys also arrived but since only four entered service, numbered 20 to 23, it may be assumed that the others were purchased to provide spare parts for the earlier survivors.

Surprisingly perhaps, there were also some trams in the form of four second-hand single-deckers from the ill-fated Dearne District Light Railways which closed in September of that year and a second-hand double-deck car, dating from 1915 from Accrington whose trams had finished in January 1932; since that system operated on 4ft width tracks there would be some regauging to take place unless the body was transferred

onto another truck. The final car to be acquired, in 1934, was another second-hand one, this being a four-wheel totally enclosed double-decker from Preston Corporation, No. 42, which had been assembled using parts from withdrawn cars in 1929 and was thus only five years old when the Preston system closed. It was allocated the highest number in the Lytham tram fleet, 56.

By now the fleet was large in comparison to the service requirements, only 32 of the 55 passenger cars being required even during the summer period and it became common for cars to be hired to Blackpool Corporation during busy periods, particularly at the time of the illuminations.

One of the four single-deckers from Dearne District, number 54, stands outside the depot whilst the former Preston car number 56 is seen in service. This was the time when Blackpool was taking the first of its striking new railcoaches and introducing a new green and cream livery. Not to be outdone Lytham now smartened up its trams with cream sweeps on the front dashes. *(STA/JNC)*

Similarly, of course, there had been times when Lytham had hired *from* Blackpool when traffic levels had required this.

In March 1933 Blackpool Corporation wanted to extend its bus route 5 from its terminus at the Halfway House to Lytham and to operate it in conjunction with Lytham St Annes Corporation. It has been suggested that the desire behind this was to foil Ribble's latest application for a service from Blackpool to Lytham but nothing came of it.

Two years later in March 1935, despite opposition from Ribble and the London, Midland & Scottish Railway Company, the Traffic Commissioners granted to the two municipalities a licence for a new joint bus service to be numbered 11 and operating from Adelaide Place, Blackpool to Lytham Square via Central Drive, St Annes Road, Halfway House, Blackpool Road, Headroomgate Road and Church Road. The new service operated via the 'back route' missing out the shopping area of St Annes. The service commenced on 7th June 1935 and was operated initially by single-deckers (see the map overleaf).

Nineteen thirty-five was to be notable for several other events. It was the year of the Royal Silver Jubilee Celebrations and to mark the occasion a special free admission ticket was issued to the children of the borough for Jubilee Day, Monday 6th May 1935. This entitled them to the following concessions :-

Lytham St Annes Trams and Buses - All day
Ashton Marine Park and Lake (Boating)
- 8am to 2pm.
Lytham Swimming Baths - 8am to 2pm.
Lytham Children - Lytham Palace Pictures
11am and 2.45pm.
Fireworks Display at the Ashton Marine Park
9pm

In this year there were further approaches from Ribble and also from Blackpool Corporation. The plan from Blackpool was to take over the complete undertaking with the intention of reconstructing the whole of the tramway as far south as St Annes and operating it as a continuation of the Promenade service and using its streamline cars. The Blackpool offer was in the sum of £116,000 to cover liabilities and to include the replacement of trams between St Annes and Lytham with modern buses. At the same time Ribble renewed the proposal, first made in 1931, to replace the trams with buses and offered to Lytham St Annes a proportion of the annual profits. Since there had never been any profits on the tramway throughout its entire life the offer must have seemed to have some merit! However, because Ribble had connections with the London, Midland & Scottish Railway Company this offer was rejected.

The proposal from Blackpool was the subject of protracted discussions before being narrowly defeated by Lytham St Annes Borough Council which now decided to abandon the whole of the tramway but to retain control of its own motor bus department. It was also resolved that there should be more co-ordination with Blackpool.

The bus intake for 1935 was again varied, and again included further second-hand purchases. A former Leyland demonstrator with distinctive cutaway rear entrance became No. 24 whilst four bonnetted Lionesses from Burnley, unwanted after the formation of Burnley, Colne & Nelson JTC, became Nos. 25-28 and were soon seen in their new role as open-toppers – again keeping up with Blackpool. Finally, three new Leylands with Burlingham bodywork became Nos. 29-31.

The event for which 1935 would most be remembered was, however, somewhat less pleasant. A 70mph storm lifted several thousand

When the wind lifted quantities of sand from the dunes onto the roadway and over the tram tracks the sweeper car was unable to tackle the problem, and good old-fashioned elbow grease and shovels were required. *(STA/JNC)*

21

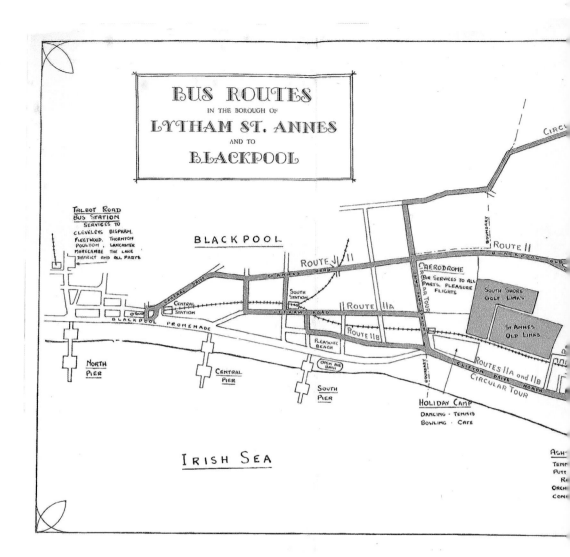

On their home territory the buses now presented a smart and quite modern appearance – especially from the back where the long bonnets of the Lionesses from Burnley are out of sight. *(STA/JNC)*

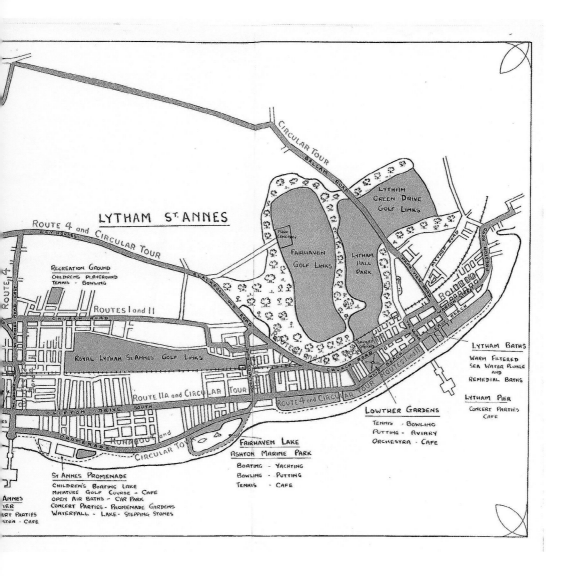

LYTHAM St. ANNES

ROUTE 4 and CIRCULAR TOUR

LYTHAM
GREEN DRIVE
GOLF LINKS

CIRCULAR TOUR
BALAAM ROAD

FAIRHAVEN
GOLF LINKS

LYTHAM
HALL
PARK

PARK CEMETERY

RECREATION GROUND
CHILDRENS PLAYGROUND
TENNIS · BOWLING

ROUTES I and II

CHURCH ROAD

ROYAL LYTHAM St. ANNES GOLF LINKS

ROUTE IIA and CIRCULAR TOUR

ROUTE 4 and CIRCULAR TOUR

CLIFTON DRIVE SOUTH

PROMENADE and
CIRCULAR TOUR

LYTHAM BATHS

WARM FILTERED
SEA WATER PLUNGE
AND
REMEDIAL BATHS

LYTHAM PIER
CONCERT PARTIES
CAFE

LOWTHER GARDENS
TENNIS · BOWLING
PUTTING · AVIARY
ORCHESTRA · CAFE

FAIRHAVEN LAKE
ASHTON MARINE PARK
BOATING · YACHTING
BOWLING · PUTTING
TENNIS · CAFE

St ANNES PROMENADE
CHILDREN'S BOATING LAKE
MINIATURE GOLF COURSE · CAFE
OPEN AIR BATHS · CAR PARK
CONCERT PARTIES · PROMENADE GARDENS
WATERFALL · LAKE · STEPPING STONES

ANNES
IER
RT PARTIES
STRA · CAFE

It was quite a different story with the trams, however. Two of Lytham's veterans rub shoulders uneasily with one of Blackpool's new monster Balloon cars at the Gynn terminus. *(STA/JNC)*

tons of sand from the dunes and deposited this mass across the tram tracks, bringing all services to a halt for three days until it had been cleared. The event which caused this was actually the 1909 Air Pageant which had been watched by thousands of spectators – on the dunes. They badly damaged the starr grass (from which Starr Gate derives its name); it never recovered, and there was then nothing to hold the sand in place so away it blew.

The previously mentioned greater co-ordination with Blackpool became effective in summer 1936 when licences were sought for an 'all year' service from Adelaide Place, Blackpool to Meadow Lane, Lytham via Central Drive and Bloomfield Road, then following the inland blue tram route of Lytham St Annes along Lytham Road, Squires Gate Lane and Clifton Drive. At the same time a seasonal service to operate at Easter, Whitsuntide and summer was commenced from Adelaide Place via South Shore to St Annes Pier. It was agreed that receipts would be returned to the authority within whose boundary they were taken, which necessitated double booking over the boundary for single journeys whilst revenue from return tickets was allocated on a *pro rata* basis to the mileage operated.

Lytham's first full sized Leyland was this former demonstrator, now No. 24 in the fleet. Its arrival marked what would be an unbroken run of Leylands of various types (save for two wartime Daimlers allocated to the undertaking in 1943/4) which lasted until 1972 (see Appendix 2). *(STA/JNC)*

With tramway replacement in mind, the first double-decker buses arrived in October 1936 and comprised two Leyland TD4c models with full fronted Leyland bodies. They were followed by three similar models in December 1936. Permission to operate the replacement bus services was granted by the Traffic Commissioners on 5th December 1936 and they took over from the trams between Lytham and St Annes on 15th December 1936. The remaining tramway services closed on 27th March 1937 except for the cars from St Annes to Gynn Square via the Promenade. The final section between Squires Gate and St Annes Square closed on 28th April 1937 with a ceremonial last journey by No. 41 driven by Councillor CH Riley JP with fares collected by Councillor JW Horsfall.

However, the one-third of a mile section of track which Lytham St Annes owned in Squires Gate Lane was retained. This formed an important link between the Starr Gate Tramway terminus of the Promenade tramway and the terminus of the Lytham Road tramway at Squires Gate. This length of track was used, under agreement, by Blackpool Corporation until 1939 and was subsequently purchased by them. It was covered over but was later uncovered and used by open toast rack cars on circular tours over the Lytham Road and Promenade tracks. Blackpool trams never operated to Lytham in passenger service though a replica tank on a tram underframe had made the journey in 1918 in connection with war

fund-raising whilst an attempt to take one of the streamlined single-deckers to Lytham resulted in a derailment on a sharp bend at Ansdell.

Also delivered in 1936 were four Leyland LT7c single-deckers, the first with body by HV Burlingham of Blackpool and the others with bodies by Leyland. Similar double- and single-deck vehicles were delivered in 1937, all with bodies by Leyland, the last four double-deckers being to the later Titan TD5c specification.

The 'c' suffix to the chassis designations for these buses signified that they were fitted with the torque converter transmission system which had recently been introduced by Leyland in an attempt to simplify driving by eliminating the need for the driver to be involved in gear changing. Buses so fitted normally carried the words 'GEARLESS BUS' on the radiator and the system appealed to municipal operators faced with increasing levels of town traffic and the need to train tram drivers to drive buses. The downside of this system is that it was less efficient in terms of fuel consumption and power output. In view of this a number of municipal operators later replaced the torque converters with standard clutch and gearbox.

The torque convertor header tank can be seen on the bulkhead and the **Gearless Bus** lettering on the radiator as number 40 poses before delivery. The change of livery is striking when compared to the ex-demonstrator in the former scheme, opposite. Number 34 from the previous batch survives in splendid condition in preservation.*(STA)*

There is, however, no record of Lytham St Annes having carried out such modification and as the last of these vehicles was not withdrawn until 1964 they must have been the last such vehicles to operate in service.

The success of the torque convertor at Lytham St Annes was due in part to the flat terrain of the area. There was, however, another factor which contributed to the longevity of these units. In order to work efficiently, the brass seals inside the units needed to have perfectly smooth faces and this was achieved by rubbing the brass faces on a flat surface using a fine lapping paste like Brasso or jewellers rouge. The other ingredient required was patience and the undertaking was fortunate in employing a fitter who was content to sit for hours or days at a time, twirling the bushes around his finger until they were polished to perfection. This man was so important to the efficient operation of the fleet that, after his 'call up' to the army in World War 2, he was released at the request of the undertaking, in order to maintain maximum availability of the fleet during wartime. It should be pointed out that since there were large numbers of forces personnel in the Blackpool area during the Second War there would have been greater Governmental co-operation than might otherwise have been the case.

By 1937 the scene was set for the basic pattern of services which was to continue for 40 years although there were changes to the Lytham to Blackpool services, some of which were necessitated by the development of Blackpool Airport as we shall see.

BTC 624

Keeping up with Blackpool was a full-time job; Burlingham had produced a striking centre-entrance full-fronted double-decker for them but Lytham preferred the rear platform. It did manage to persuade Leyland to modify its new double-deck body, however, no small achievement in itself, and this full-fronted design was the result when the tram replacement vehicles started to arrive. As Lytham's first double-deckers they made quite a considerable impact – especially on the joint services into Blackpool! *(STA/JNC)*

4 – Wartime

During the Second World War there were restrictions on the purchase of new buses with the allocations strictly controlled by the Ministry of War Transport. Leyland Motors was engaged in manufacture for the war effort and was not allowed to manufacture buses. Lytham St Annes was allowed to purchase two new double-deckers, one in 1943 and the other in 1944. Both were Daimler CWA6 models with bodies by Duple built to the Standard Utility Wartime Specification.

Services were affected by restrictions on the supply of fuel and there were also restrictions with regard to vehicle lighting, leading to the masking of interior lights and headlights. This combined with the elimination of street lighting made the driving of buses a hazardous occupation during the hours of darkness. Fortunately, in those days there was not the amount of traffic that there is on the roads today.

In January 1940, as a result of heavy snowfall, there was considerable disruption to traffic, an event which the press referred to as 'The Great Transport Hold-up'. The Fylde Coast was cut off for almost a week apart from a daily bus service to Preston. Service 11 between Blackpool and Lytham was diverted along Squires Gate Lane

The unmistakable outline of the Duple bodywork on this Daimler points clearly to its status as a wartime utility bus, needed to help with moving the large numbers of forces personnel in the area. Number 23, the second of a pair, is seen here in post-war days. *(RM)*

and Clifton Drive North to operate via St Annes Square and St Annes Road East and rejoin its normal route at Church Road.

Developments at Blackpool airport also brought changes to services. RAF Coastal Command took over the Airport and immediately closed Blackpool Road North in order to provide additional runways and to accommodate its Wellington bomber factory. As a result of this the diversion of route 11 became permanent and a new service numbered 11C was commenced in February 1940 operating from Adelaide Street, Blackpool to St Annes Pier via Common Edge Road, Division Lane, Headroomgate Road, St Annes Road East and St Annes Road West. There had previously been a route 11C operated only by Lytham St Annes as a short working of route 11 between Adelaide Street and Lindsey Avenue, St Annes. The new service 11C was operated by single-deck buses until the 'fifties when it became double-deck operated. Although it was a joint service, it was operated only by Blackpool vehicles.

It is pleasing to record that the staff at the undertaking were so well thought of for the work they did during wartime, that a collection by the people of Lytham St Annes was used to purchase two top quality snooker tables which remained in the staff rest room until closure of the company.

With the end of the war in sight, preparations began for a return to peacetime operation though there would be many difficulties to face in the austerity years ahead.

5 – Postwar Developments

Lytham St Annes Corporation had placed forward orders during the war with Leyland Motors and was thus early in the queue for delivery of new vehicles, six Leyland PD1 double-deckers with Leyland bodies arriving in 1946. They were painted in the post-war livery of mainly blue, with white relief. The halcyon days of the cream livery had sadly passed.

In November Manager JC Fairchild retired. He had taken over the reins way back in 1929, had built up a more modern bus fleet, seen the withdrawal of the trams, modified the livery and guided the undertaking through the difficult war years.

His successor was his deputy, W Ashton, who had joined the undertaking in 1910 and was thus well versed in the affairs of the Borough. He inherited a sound operation and remained in post until his retirement in 1954.

A further six Leyland-bodied double-deckers arrived in 1948, these being to the then recently introduced PD2/1 specification fitted with the more powerful engine.

As from 1st June 1950 the maximum width for a bus was increased to 8ft and the maximum length for a vehicle on two axles was increased to 27ft; the 1951 deliveries took advantage of this change in legislation resulting in the arrival of five Leyland PD2/12 double-deckers, again with Leyland bodies. The arrival of these 17 new vehicles between 1946 and 1951 resulted in an increase in fleet size because during this period only three vehicles had been withdrawn.

Service 11 with its variants continued to be the backbone of the system and it had been the intention of Blackpool Corporation to build a new road round the back of the Airport to cater for heavy traffic for which Division Lane was considered unsuitable. This had been delayed because of wartime restrictions but materialised in 1954 as Queensway. Service 11C was then diverted along this road and although this was a joint service it continued to be operated entirely by Blackpool vehicles.

The other significant event relevant to our story from 1954 was the retirement of W Ashton who had been in charge since 1946. Having started his career in 1910 he must have known the system and its idiosyncracies inside out.

His successor, Ronald C Armstrong, joined from Morecambe & Heysham where he had been Deputy Manager for the last three years. His career mirrored that of Mr Ashton, something which clearly appealed to the interviewing panel. He had joined M&H as a general clerk in 1927,

Shown in St Annes Square in July 1964 is No. 19, a Leyland-bodied Leyland PD1 one of the first post-war vehicles to be delivered in 1946. It remained in service until September 1972 and is now preserved. *(BD)*

Leyland PD2 No. 12 dating from 1948 emerges from Headroomgate Road on to St Annes Road with St Annes Parish Church in the background. The snow, a rare occurrence on the Fylde Coast, is noteworthy. *(JNC)*

Photographed outside St Annes Parish Church in May 1950, 1937 Leyland TD5c No. 50 shows off its later blue livery. *(RM)*

This scene in Lytham in the early fifties shows 1937 Leyland LT7c No. 44 operating on service 4 to St Annes. The Gearless Bus lettering has gone from the radiator front. *(RM)*

A post-war view of the depot taken from Squires Gate Lane showing the gardens and two of the pre-war Leyland Lion single-deckers which had been converted to open-top in 1946 by Blackpool Coachcraft. It is thought that the photograph was taken following the fitting of new roller shutter doors. *(JNC)*

1957 Burlingham-bodied Leyland Tiger Cub No. 54 makes its way through Lytham Square while one of the batch of 1937 Leyland-bodied Leyland TD4c double-deckers, partially hidden behind the trees and still with torque converter transmission, awaits its next departure to Blackpool. *(JNC)*

Number 61 was one of five Leyland PD2 models with bodywork by Northern Counties Motor & Engineering Company Ltd of Wigan delivered in 1957. It was photographed for the coachbuilder on completion in a location regularly used, just off Wigan Lane near their works, for this purpose. Modern day traffic levels would make this impossible. *(JNC)*

rising to Chief Clerk by 1939. He spent five years in war service before returning to his previous post for another two years. He was then promoted to Chief Assistant, and in 1951 became deputy General Manager.

The first underfloor-engined single-deckers arrived in the fleet in 1957 when three Leyland Tiger Cub chassis with bodies by HV Burlingham were purchased. In the same year a further five new double-deckers were purchased. Leyland was again favoured with the chassis order but a new supplier for the bodies had to be found as Leyland, the main supplier of all peacetime buses, had ceased body manufacture. As a result of this, the order was placed with Northern Counties Motor and Engineering Company of Wigan.

Ticketing Arrangements on Jointly Operated Services

Reference has previously been made to ticketing arrangements on services operated jointly by Lytham St Annes Corporation and Blackpool Corporation. At the request of the Traffic Commissioners, it was eventually resolved with effect from 1st October 1958 when a pooling system was established. Prior to this double-booking at the boundary had been involved

under a system which has been described as 'the tail wagging the dog'. It incorporated a number of unusual features in addition to re-booking at the boundary. There were a few through return fares for which the revenue was divided in agreed proportions and which were fixed when the services terminated at Central Station, Blackpool. When the services were extended to Talbot Road Bus Station problems arose. Both operators used TIM ticket machines and the administrative arrangements provided for the use of certain values on the machine to be used only for return tickets. For example, on Blackpool machines a 1s return was always made up of two 6d tickets married together, but a 6d single was always issued as two 3d tickets married together. In this way, everything on the 6d counter could be shared with Lytham St Annes. When the services were

31

extended to Talbot Road Bus Station, returns could only be issued as far as Central Station but their holders were allowed to book a 1d excess to cover the extended section of the route. This of course created extra work for conductors and confusion for passengers, many of whom were visitors. There was also an added complication in that returns were only issued for adults. This meant that an adult with a child travelling from St Annes to Blackpool Talbot Road and return would be provided with an adult return from St Annes to Blackpool Central Station at which point it would be necessary to book a 1d excess fare to Talbot Road. For the child it was necessary to book a single to the boundary and then another single to Talbot Road. The same procedure would be followed for the return journey. The conductors must have been relieved when the pooling arrangement was introduced in 1958, not only would it reduce their work but no doubt saved many arguments with passengers from other areas where pooling had been the norm for many years.

Number 65, below, a Metro-Cammell-bodied Leyland PD2 dating from 1960, is shown in St Annes Square heading for Squires Gate on service 1 on 21st July 1970. This design was notable for the increased use of fibreglass (grp) in the body construction, especially in the front and rear domes. The design may be compared to the vehicle on the facing page, number 68, a 1964 Leyland PD2 with body by Massey Brothers, which is shown entering St Annes Square on service 3 to Lytham Square in May 1970. Amongst many differences the equal sized windows on both decks may be compared to the shallower upper deck ones fitted to the MCW version. The St Helens front bonnet arrangement (so-called after being designed to meet that operator's preferences) is well-suited to the Massey body whilst the earlier flat and uninspiring design seems at home on the Orion. *(BD)*

6 – The Sixties

Six new double-deckers arrvied in 1960 with Leyland again being favoured with the chassis order. The bodies were a new departure for Lytham St Annes being by Metropolitan Cammell Weymann to their 'Orion' style. At this time operators were concerned about falling passenger numbers and rising fuel costs and this body style had been introduced as a 'lightweight' design in an attempt to improve fuel consumption and minimise capital costs. The proportions were rather ungainly but the appearance was helped by the attractive blue and white livery used by Lytham St Annes. This advantage was, however, to be lost when the brighter livery with increased area of white

was introduced in 1973, as illustrated in the photographic section. Number 62 from this batch of vehicles was painted in an all gold livery for a few weeks in 1972 to commemorate the 'Golden Jubilee' of the amalgamation of Lytham and St Annes to form the Borough of Lytham St Annes. It was then painted white and provided with advertisements for the Jubilee events and later used to promote events in connection with the 'Year of the Child'.

Prototype Leyland Atlantean 398 JTB was on loan from Leyland Motors in August 1960.

Further new double-deckers arrived in 1964, again being on Leyland PD2 chassis. However, the bodies were a complete contrast to the 1960 delivery being by Massey Brothers of Wigan to their elegant styling and were very attractive vehicles. They were the first double-deckers in the

fleet to have front-entrances and these were fitted with sliding doors.

In his Annual Report dated 31st March 1969 the general manager, Mr RC Armstrong, reported a deficit of £4,221 against a record income of £201,719 compared to £192,243 for the previous year. The increased income was due to improved trading during the holiday season and increased fares introduced on 28th October 1968. The deficit was attributed to the delay before increased fares could be implemented and also the wage increase of £1 per week to staff which had been back-dated over a period of twelve months, the retrospective payment alone amounting to £7,250. During the twelve months the total mileage operated on all services was 1,086,744 compared to 1,124,342 for the previous year. The reduction was attributed to the curtailment of unremunerative services. The total number of staff employed was 140 and the rolling stock total was 37 including two vehicles noted as 'obsolete and withdrawn from service'. It was noted that six vehicles were on order and that these were likely to replace eight of the 56-seater double-deckers. The vehicle testing station operated on behalf of the Ministry of Transport dealt with 1,679 vehicles, a considerable increase on the total of 693 in the previous year.

The year 1969 saw the introduction of the first rear-engined single-deckers in the form of three Leyland Panther PSUR1 models with dual-doorway bodies by Northern Counties, purchased to replace double-deckers which required a conductor, on lightly trafficked routes. They were followed the following year by three Leyland Atlantean PDR1/1 rear-engined double-deckers also with bodies by Northern Counties to what was generally referred to as the 'Nottingham' design. They were part of an order 'tacked-on' to one for Nottingham, basically to that operator's normal specification, thereby speeding up delivery and keeping the purchase price down.

These were the first municipally owned rear-engined double-deckers on the Fylde Coast and their arrival allowed further expansion of one person operation, although initially, they were operated with conductors.

The last new vehicles to be received by Lytham St Annes Corporation marked a departure from Leyland which had been the sole chassis supplier since the mid-thirties apart from the two Daimlers delivered in wartime. The order comprised six Seddon RU rear-engined single-deckers with bodies by Seddon's subsidiary bodybuilding company, Pennine Coachcraft.

This vehicle was an attempt by Seddon to provide a rear-engined single-decker similar to the very successful Bristol RE which, though it had initially been restricted to operators within

Northern Counties-bodied Leyland Panther No. 71 passes over the railway bridge at Ansdell Station. *(JNC)*

Picking up passengers outside the original Marks and Spencer in Blackpool, in September 1971 is Atlantean No. 76, one of the Nottingham-styled vehicles. *(RM)*

Number 47, a Seddon RU, displays the 'Fylde' fleetname as it passes the Independent Methodist Church on Central Drive, Blackpool on 28th June 1975. *(BD)*

the nationalised Tilling and Scottish Groups, had become a firm favourite in many other fleets. It was eventually killed off by Leyland in an attempt to force more sales for the integral Leyland National single-decker, a move which caused great resentment and eventually lost BL much business.

The Seddon design was not very successful, the largest batch of 100 going to Crosville Motor Services and the problems which that company had with those vehicles have been well documented. The fact that they were delivered in 1972 and that withdrawal commenced in 1978

and was complete by 1983 speaks volumes, although it has to be said that the first withdrawal was due to accident damage. It may be recalled that for Crosville the one redeeming feature was that the Gardner engines could be recovered and fitted as replacements in their Leyland Nationals. The biter bit?

The remark has also been passed that the Seddons were 'no worse than the Leyland Panthers' which, since that model was not Leyland's most successful product, is hardly a ringing endorsement.

A Complicated Vehicle Order

In March 1973 Mr John Nye was appointed General Manager of the undertaking. He had begun his career with Liverpool CTD in 1943, moving to St Helens in 1954 as Senior Schedules Clerk, then to Accrington as Traffic Superintendent before going to Burnley, Colne and Nelson as Deputy GM in 1971, the position he left to join Lytham. On his arrival he was advised that six Leyland Atlantean chassis had been ordered but that no order had been placed for bodies due to the fact that there had been no response to the invitation to tender for the bodies. New tender documents were prepared and sent out to the recognised bodybuilders of the time. During the tender period Mr Reg Brindle, the representative for the Yeates dealership in Loughborough, who actually lived in Lytham, asked if Yeates could tender for the bodies and this was agreed. When the tenders were received, the only tender was from Yeates, based on bodies built by Willowbrook. In the circumstances the Council had no alternative but to accept this tender and an order was placed with Yeates. After a lapse of time and with no progress being made on the body contract, Yeates requested permission to transfer the order to Northern Counties Motor and Engineering Company of Wigan who would possibly have received the order in the first place if they had submitted a tender. It was then suggested by Yeates that Northern Counties should build the frames complete with the exterior panelling and Willowbrook would carry out the interior finishing. This was agreed and the vehicles were delivered in February and March 1975, over two years after the ordering of the chassis and carrying both Willowbrook and Northern Counties body numbers but badged as Willowbrook. By the time of their arrival, the undertaking had passed to the newly formed Fylde Borough Council.

For several years no timetable or fares table booklet had been issued but in view of the forthcoming change of ownership it was decided to issue a 'last momento' . This took the form of a Commemorative Time and Fare Table booklet which was issued on 29th October 1973. It was priced at 5p and in addition to time and fare details it included a brief history of the undertaking and four photographs. These were tram No. 6 dating from 1922, Guy 'B' type bus No. 3 which entered service in 1923, double-decker No. 47 which operated from 1937 to 1963 and Seddon single-decker No. 45 which had recently entered service in 1972. A list of the services included in this booklet is given in Appendix 4.

The first of the 1975 Willowbrook/Northern Counties Leyland Atlanteans is handed over by Reg Brindle of Yeates to the Chairman of the Transport Committee watched by Martin Montano (representing Duple, owners of Willowbrook), John Nye, (General Manager), Councillor Joyce and Bob Hatten (Rolling Stock Superintendent). *(JNC)*

7 – Fylde Borough Council Transport

The Borough of Fylde was formed with effect from 1st April 1974 and the undertaking was renamed Fylde Borough Council Transport. Apart from the change of fleetname the livery continued as the brighter version introduced by Lytham St Annes Corporation but a mustard yellow band was later introduced. By now the fleet was ageing with many of the immediate postwar buses still in service, a situation which had been compounded by the delay in the delivery of new Leyland Atlanteans related in the previous chapter. In addition there was a need to effect economies, mainly through the introduction of one person operation. It was also decided to develop the private hire business and to this end two Plaxton-bodied Leyland Leopard coaches were purchased in June 1974.

In addition to the new Leyland Atlanteans, the year 1975 also saw the arrival of another Plaxton-bodied Leyland Leopard coach and five Bristol RE rear-engined single-deckers with bodies by Eastern Coachworks of Lowestoft. These were the first Bristols to be operated by the undertaking and had been ordered by Lytham St Annes. The choice was not surprising as the Bristol RE had gained a reputation of being the best rear-engined single-decker on the market and these vehicles gave good service, remaining until 1993.

For the next few years the standard delivery for double-deckers became the Leyland Atlantean with body by Northern Counties together with a number of coaches, mainly Leyland Leopards with bodies by Duple or Plaxton but including a Volvo B58 and a Leyland Tiger, all as detailed in the Fleet Summary.

With the build-up of the coach fleet together with the use of high back seating in the Leyland Atlanteans and the Bristol REs, opportunities

Photographed in St Annes Square in June 1974 and carrying the recently applied 'Fylde' fleetname is No. 8, a handsome Leyland-bodied Leyland PD2 dating from 1951 and closely followed by an example of the ubiquitous Morris Minor van. *(RM)*

The first two coaches to be purchased arrived in 1974 and comprised Plaxton-bodied Leyland Leopards numbered 43 and 44, as seen here. *(JNC)*

arose for the hiring of vehicles to Ribble Motor Services and to National Express for use on express services. This was particularly relevant in the seventies when 'Wakes Weeks' were still in vogue and as a result vehicles from the Fylde fleet could be seen operating in many parts of the country and particularly on the well known X60 service between Blackpool and Manchester. This service, with a 15 minutes frequency, plus duplicates, on summer Saturdays was known as the most frequent express bus service in the world until National Bus Company managed to kill it off.

On one occasion National Express requested a coach with driver to report to Coliseum Coach Station, Blackpool. On arrival the duty inspector had no work for the coach and directed the driver to Preston at which point he was directed to Manchester. The inspector at Manchester had no work, but wanting to be helpful said that Birmingham was sure to have need of the coach and directed the driver there. Birmingham did not however need the coach and the driver was sent on to London Victoria where again the was no work. The inspector told the driver to take a break and then return home. It seems that no one could recall whether or not Fylde received payment for all the mileage.

In order to speed up the conversion to one person operation a number of secondhand vehicles were purchased. The first, arriving in 1977, comprised a batch of six Leyland Atlantean PDR1 models, dating from 1964, from Merseyside PTE which had been taken over from Liverpool City Transport on formation of the PTE. The bodies were by Metropolitan Cammell Carriage and Wagon Company and had been designed in conjunction with Liverpool City Transport who were not satisfied with the standard Metropolitan Cammell body which was being offered for rear engined double-deckers. This was to be a forerunner of things to come, but more of that later. The arrival of these six vehicles allowed the move to one person operation to be accelerated, although one of them was not used in service but as a source of spares.

No further secondhand double-deckers were purchased in the years 1978 to 1985, apart from an open-top Leyland Atlantean bought from Lancaster City Transport in 1985. Three Leyland Leopards with dual-purpose Weymann bodies arrived from Ribble Motor Services in 1979. New vehicles were Leyland Atlanteans with Northern Counties bodies and a solitary single-deck service bus in the form of a Leyland Tiger with Duple body and five coaches.

During 1982/3 the finances of Fylde Borough Transport were not looking good and talks were held with Blackpool Transport to consider either

Bristol RE No. 40 shows its two shades of blue livery in St Annes in May 1991 as it heads for Wesham. The via blind has been removed and replaced by fixed signwriting encouraging would-be passengers to *TRAVEL WITH US ON A FRIENDLY BLUE BUS. (RM)*

With a Blackpool 'Balloon' double-deck tram in the background, Northern Counties-bodied Leyland Atlantean number 99, passes the Manchester Hotel and proceeds along Lytham Road, Blackpool towards St Annes and Lytham in August 1983. The Coliseum coach station and Corporation's Rigby Road tram sheds are to the right with just the merest hint of the kerb showing the way in. *(HP)*

Ex-Merseyside Leyland Atlantean Number 89 was displaying the latest style of livery with upswept yellow band when photographed at the depot in June 1982. *(RM)*

In the upper view open-topper No. 89 travels north along Blackpool Promenade on 2nd July 1987 with the 'Blue Bus Billy' fleetname. The treatment of the upper-deck on the former Salford vehicle is unusual, to say the least. *(RM)*

Number 43, in the lower view, a Leyland Tiger with Duple Dominant bus body, leaves Talbot Road Bus Station for Squires Gate on 14th May 1988 followed by Ribble Olympian 2145 en route to Preston. *(BD)*

a merger with Blackpool or for Blackpool to take over the undertaking. However, history repeated itself and Fylde decided to continue with bus operation. During the early part of 1983 a new joint working arrangement was negotiated between Fylde and Blackpool to improve the co-ordination of bus services in the two areas. This resulted in Blackpool's 22/22A service being extended from its southern terminus at the Halfway House to operate from Cleveleys to Lytham via St Annes and co-ordination of services 11/11A along Lytham Road particularly during evenings and Sundays.

8 – Deregulation

The publication of the 1985 Transport Act was to have a major effect on passenger transport operators throughout the country. On the one hand it proposed the privatisation of the National Bus Company and on the other hand, the deregulation of local bus services, thus removing the protection from direct competition which operators had enjoyed under the 1930 Transport Act. In practice, this meant that operators, both established and new, could register any local service which they believed could be operated commercially (at a profit). Operators were no longer allowed to cross subsidise services and only where the Transport Authority (County Council or Passenger Transport Executive) considered that the level of service did not meet a particular social need, was it allowed discretion to invite tenders for the provision of the service or journeys concerned. From the same time the Restrictive Trade Practices Act 1976 was now to apply to bus services and so meant that the operation of a joint service by two or more operators, or any joint fares marketing schemes, needed to be registered with the Office of Fair Trading. In the early days, most of these were deemed to be anti-competitive.

Local Authorities were required to divest themselves of their transport undertakings, either to form separate 'arms length' limited liability companies, or to sell to private companies. Faced with the possibility of new operators registering what they saw as profitable services, many local authorities decided to sell. Fylde Borough Council decided to retain control of its transport undertaking and an 'arms length company', Fylde Borough Transport Limited, was formed and commenced operation on 'D' day 26th October 1986.

Lancashire County Council was very much against the 1985 Transport Act and published a series of leaflets in January 1985 covering various areas of the County under the general heading 'Your bus service is under attack'. On the back of the leaflet there was a letter from Councillor Mrs Louise Ellman, Chair of Lancashire County Council, in which she suggested that the people of Lancashire might like to contact their Member of Parliament and voice their concerns over the proposed changes. Despite this, the Bill was passed and came into force on 26th October 1986. Prior to this, all operators were required to register with the Traffic Commissioner, by 26th February 1986, details of all services which they intended to operate commercially from Deregulation Day. Details of all these services were listed in a special edition of Notices and Proceedings dated 27th March 1986. Fylde Borough Transport published a timetable booklet effective from 26th October 1986 and services included in this booklet are listed in Appendix 5.

Timetable issued at the commencement of deregulation. *(BD)*

Fylde Borough Transport Limited

The passing of the 1985 Transport Act meant that the co-operation agreed between Fylde and Blackpool in 1983 was short lived and had to cease as it would have been regarded as anti-competitive.

The operating name 'Blue Buses' was introduced.

Because of the close proximity of Blackpool Transport Services Limited, as Blackpool Transport had become, and Ribble Motor Services Limited a policy decision was reached not to expand local services in a way that could have been regarded as provocative. With this in mind, it was estimated that it would be possible to operate with 32 buses. As a way forward, Fylde tendered for contract work with Lancashire County Council and was very successful with the result

that there was a requirement for 40 buses rather than 32. The ability to win this work arose from paying attention to detail with regard to finances, operations and maintenance, thus keeping costs per mile as low as possible.

Additional vehicles had to be sourced quickly and as a contact had been established with Kingston upon Hull City Transport, this source was used for the majority of additional vehicles required over the next five years or so. Without the need for meetings with Transport Committees, treasurers etc., secondhand vehicles could be obtained quickly. Furthermore, as the Hull livery was very similar to that at Fylde, the vehicles were able to operate at Fylde within a week and looked very much 'at home' without the need for repainting.

Whilst the ex-Hull Leyland Atlanteans fitted

into the fleet most readily, the Roe bodies were a new breed. Very soon it was discovered that the steel framework, hidden under the panels could be non-existent. A foot placed on the inside of the waist rails would soon show the flexibility where the framework had rusted away. However, a good team of one coachbuilder and one welder could replace the whole side between the axles within one week.

On Sunday 21st June 1992, No. 72 leaves Preston Bus Station on a Lancashire County Council Contract on service 29 to Frenchwood. The Northern Counties-bodied Atlantean has been reregistered with an Irish mark, disguising the vehicle's true age where contract work was involved and a limit on the age of the bus was usually imposed. *(BD)*

Ex-Hull Leyland Atlantean No. 126 still retained the centre doorway in its Roe bodywork when photographed in Blackpool in September 1988. *(RM)*

Although all the Hull Atlanteans came at a very good price, one particular AN68 was an excellent buy. The top deck rear had been badly fire damaged and it was minus a power pack but for a very low cost it was purchased, repaired and fitted with a spare engine and gearbox. This restoration did not take place immediately and the vehicle stood in the yard for some time until it could be taken into the workshop. Even then work could only be carried out spasmodically due to other commitments. By the time the bodywork had been completed, a power pack became available in an unexpected way as detailed later and this was fitted. Looking splendid both inside and outside, No. 129 made its debut working an illuminations tour. However, crossing the tram tracks at Manchester Square, soot showered down from every joint on the top deck. Fortunately this was prior to the picking up of passengers at Gynn Square.

Blue Buses would have continued to grow by gaining contracts, had not Blackpool registered routes in St Annes using their Volkswagen minibuses. Fylde responded to this with six Dodge S56 minibuses with Northern Counties bodies which were used to operate a Blackpool Promenade service in 1987, fifty years since the last blue tram had operated on the Promenade tracks. At the end of the season, the minibuses were used to open a Blackpool to Cleveleys service which, being successful, led to the purchase of more minibuses for the 1988 season. This batch was more aesthetically pleasing, having a Northern Counties-designed fibreglass front, disc brakes and a Fylde-fitted aluminium gearbox oil cooler. This item increased gearbox life beyond the previous two to three months to a respectable two years. At the end of the season the Cleveleys services were extended to Marton. This led to a further and last order for minibuses, now longer and heavier than the previous batch, so that along with previous modifications, the fitting of Telma electric retarders increased brake pad life.

In the meantime, Blackpool had started operating extra buses over common sections of route and operating on the 193 service. The result was that with more buses acquired from Hull, Blue Buses commenced operation on Blackpool services including Nos. 6 and 14, with more buses on the 11/11A service which was common with Blackpool for much of the route. By now the whole area was heavily over bussed and the Blue Buses fleet strength had risen to 98 and with ancillary vehicles was over 100, well in excess of the 32 anticipated in 1986 at the time of Deregulation.

As well as the vehicles from Hull, there were other secondhand purchases from Greater Manchester Transport in the form of Leyland Atlanteans with Northern Counties bodies and three Daimler Fleetlines with Roe bodies from Grimsby Cleethorpes Transport. These three vehicles entered service in their Grimsby Cleethorpes, Brown and Cream livery and carrying stickers stating 'Blue Buses' which brought forth much comment. Although the Roe bodies on these vehicles were identical to those on the ex-Hull vehicles, they were in excellent

Number 102, one of the first batch of minibuses, is shown in Beachcomber livery on Blackpool Promenade on 31st August 1987. *(RM)*

This former Greater Manchester Northern Counties-bodied Leyland Atlantean No. 62 is shown in brilliant sunshine at Blackpool, South Shore in August 1994 with its original destination display now replaced as seen. *(MB)*

condition due to the framework having been sprayed with wax oil. However, the heavy steering and the heavy accelerator action associated with the Gardner engines made them unpopular with drivers. The ex-Manchester AN68 Leyland Atlanteans being more standard in chassis and body type were more readily accepted, especially so because they were fitted with power assisted steering. Fylde modelled the modified destination display for these Atlanteans on that which had been used by Leeds City Transport.

Two Leyland Atlanteans were purchased from Clyde Coast Services Limited of Ardrossan in 1990. One of these reached Squires Gate successfully but the other developed a knock in the angle drive gears which became progressively worse until it was decided to park it on the hard shoulder of the M6. Using the back up staff car as transport the personnel made their way to the

Motorway Services to await the arrival of the Blue Buses recovery truck. Once hitched up, steady progress was made although by now it was after midnight. Descending the hills below Tebay, the bus received a shunt to the rear from a fast moving 40 tonne truck. As the coupling equipment was damaged a further wait ensued for a private recovery truck which, using a suspended tow, arrived at the depot at 5.30am, over 24 hours after setting out. The Atlantean, although a write off after the accident, provided the power unit for the ex-Hull Atlantean No. 129 mentioned earlier.

Promenade Service Open-Toppers

With all these buses dashing up and down the coast something had to give and so common sense allowed a degree of scaling back which left Blue Buses with a number of spare vehicles.

In order to avoid the purchase of more minibuses

Number 53, one of the former Hull Atlanteans, shows its half open-top arrangement as it heads south through Talbot Square, Blackpool on 18th August 1993. *(RM)*

for the Promenade service and the need to find even more new routes for them in the autumn, thoughts turned to the surplus double-deckers. To provide a new identity, the service was rebranded from the minibus 'Beachcomber' to become 'Coastliner' and later 'Rollercoaster'. For almost every operation in summer, the livery was varied using the company's blue, white and yellow colours, as used on the minibuses, to keep a fresh image. A further development was to use open-top buses. The first of these was DBA 227C, a Leyland Atlantean PDR1 with Metro Cammell body which had originally been in the fleet of Salford City Transport before passing to Lancaster City Transport from whom it had been purchased in open-top form. It had been the last vehicle to enter service with Fylde Borough Transport prior to the commencement of operations by Fylde Borough Transport Limited. It was a full open-topper but as this gave no protection in adverse weather conditions, a local joiner made a hardwood frame to fit over the front part of the top deck including the staircase. This was covered with transparent polycarbonate to provide 'all weather' protection to the front half of the top deck. So successful was it that, when other buses were converted, only the rear half of the top deck was exposed, the style setting a country-wide trend. As the Promenade service was primarily a holiday service, fun themes were developed such as fancy complicated mouse traps painted upstairs on bus 52. Bus 54 carried a jig saw with one piece missing which was hidden among painted skipping ropes and whips and tops on another bus for children to find. Alas, one summer the bus carrying the missing piece did not run due to a major fault; there must have been much searching that year. The last conversion was done in the style of a Paris bus with the windows removed in the rear half of the top deck but with the roof remaining in place. The inside of the roof of this section carried a 6ft square painting of a snakes and ladders and before it was fitted into place, the staff who created it played a knock out competition with it. Are all men little boys at heart?

The promenade buses were sign written, advertising details of the route. When one of these buses was hired by a local church to head a procession around the area, it was reputed that a combination of the church banners and the advertising details read :- *Jesus Saves - anywhere along the Promenade for 50p*.

Roe-bodied former Hull Atlantean No. 122, now in half open-top form and in the two shades of blue livery but not doing much business, proceeds down Talbot Road, Blackpool, into Talbot Square in May 1989. *(RM)*

9 – Seagull Coaches

In parallel with the developments in bus services there were also developments on the coaching side of the business. In 1986 a number of coaches were operating in the fleet under the 'Blue Buses' banner. These consisted of a Leyland Tiger with Duple Laser 2 body, several Leyland Leopards with Duple bodies and one with a Plaxton body, all with pneumocyclic semi-automatic gearboxes. There was also one Volvo B58 with Duple body and synchromesh gearbox. Most of the work carried out by this small fleet comprised private hire and school trips with some loan duties to National Express. The private hire side did increase and at one stage accounted for about 25% of the business. There were contracts with the army from Weeton Camp and an organisation named Nord Anglia for the conveyance of foreign students at holiday times.

During 1987 the owner of Seagull Coaches offered Blue Buses the option to purchase and the deal was completed whereby three further Leyland Leopards all with Duple bodies joined the fleet in April 1988. In addition to the vehicles there were three Promenade booking offices. Two of the coaches had semi- automatic gearboxes whilst the third had a six speed manual ZF gear box which had been made available in the Leopard after the demise of the AEC Reliance. This third vehicle was originally numbered 44 but later received the number 30 from the ex-Kelvin Scottish Duple-bodied Leyland Leopard which was renumbered 36 after which it became surplus to requirements

and was withdrawn. At this time the condition of the cab of the Ford 'D' recovery vehicle was giving cause for concern. This together with a shortage of drivers with a licence to drive coaches with a manual gearbox set off a train of actions in which the semi-automatic gearbox from coach 36 was transferred to coach 30 and No. 36 received the ZF manual gearbox from No. 30. No. 36 was then converted to a recovery vehicle receiving fleet No. 159. The bodywork to the rear of the back axle together with a further section of bodywork involving the roof and one window bay were removed leaving a flat bed at the rear. A housing for the tow bar, towing hook, amber flashing light and short wave radio completed the job, apart from a notch cut from the dash to allow engagement of the third gear.

Of the Promenade booking offices, Wellington Road was the main and busiest outlet and was very quickly rebuilt as a modern booking hall closer to the sea front. It included toilets for the disabled, ramp access and central heating. There was a grand opening in the spring with 'Ken Barlow' (William Roache) of Coronation Street cutting the ribbon. St Chads booking office, oddly sited at Crystal Road, was a timber sentry box enabling one person to sit inside and issue tickets to people outside. The box had been patched and repatched over the years but it had proved very difficult to

Long-established Blackpool coach operator, Seagull Coaches, was purchased in April 1988 and the deal included three coaches, all Leyland Leopards with Duple bodies. Number 31 is shown here at the depot in August 1988. It and sister vehicle No. 32 were new to Greater Manchester Transport in 1974. *(RM)*

The acquisition of Seagull provided some engineering opportunities – here former Plaxton-bodied coach number 42 is seen with the late Ken Martin at the wheel after stripping off the coachwork in preparation for rebodying. *(MS)*

Duple-bodied ULS 653T is seen after rebuilding as a breakdown vehicle and renumbering to No. 159. *(MS)*

Corporation blue, which also became the standard for the relief lines on the coaches.

With the acquisition of Seagull, Blue Buses could tap into the holiday market and set up a full excursion programme along with tours of the illuminations. One of the most popular excursions was to Granada Studios using two 33ft long Leyland Atlanteans Nos. 24 and 25 which had coach seating and were capable of 60mph. Using these two double-deck coaches up to five times per week, Seagull gained the top award for taking the most customers to Granada almost every season.

In April 1987 coach No. 42 was returned after being on long term loan to Southend Borough Transport Limited and in October 1987 it was decided to remove the body, overhaul the chassis and have a new Duple 320 body fitted and this was undertaken in April 1988. The arrangement created a very pleasing and useful coach which, finished in Seagull livery with Irish registration number, passed as 'new' coach No. 26. The following year another Leyland Leopard No. 36 was dealt with in similar manner becoming No. 28. Due to a mistake, No. 28 had a single piece windscreen rather than the two piece windscreen as fitted to No. 26. There was a plan in hand for a third Leyland Leopard to be similarly dealt with but Plaxton purchased Duple and they were not interested in rebodying existing chassis.

In February 1991, two years after the Berlin Wall had been knocked down, coach No. 27 was used for a trip to Kaliz and Warsaw in Poland. Twenty teenagers from the 'Youth for Christ' movement were taken to experience the culture difference between east and west. They also

obtain planning permission to replace it. However, eventually after an appeal the box was replaced with a much smarter fibreglass unit of similar size. Another booking office was at Commercial Street near the 'O Be Joyful' public house at Waterloo Road. This was rented and was not easy to see from the Promenade, its only claim to fame being that it was once the outlet for the Marshall of Blackpool Coach Company. Unfortunately, the new 1988 building at Wellington Road and the new St Chads sentry box are no longer there but the original old Wellington Road office is now incorporated as a single storey building at the northern end of the Lyndene Hotel complex. The Commercial Street building still exists.

For one season, Seagull Coaches and the coaches of Blue Buses worked in two separate liveries with separate fleet names but then came together in 1989, in one brand as 'Seagull Coaches'. The new livery, based on coach No. 27 was Bachelor Blue relieved by three dark blue lines at lower level, the dark blue being that used on the bus fleet. Post 1993 the coach livery was changed from Bachelor Blue to Fresco Blue and at the same time the dark blue on the bus fleet was changed to the original Lytham St Annes

provided the help needed to manually unload the food, clothes and medical aid taken along. No. 27 performed perfectly on the 2000 miles round trip and despite having encountered thick snow and temperatures of minus 20 degrees, only one stop light bulb had to be replaced. The people of Kaliz benefitted from this trip which had been made possible by generous donations from many Blue Buses suppliers and individuals.

In an effort to engage in the touring market a DAF SB 3000 coach with Van Hool body, complete with toilet, was purchased in 1992. However, this market was well catered for in the area and despite

much effort, Seagull only managed to gain a toe hold in the touring business. After two seasons the company reverted back to day excursion work and two further coaches were purchased in 1993 from Shearings. These were Leyland Tigers with Plaxton bodies and incorporated Cummins L10 engines and hydraulically operated gearboxes. The two coaches took the numbers 24 and 25 previously carried by coach-seated Leyland Atlanteans which were renumbered 44 and 45. Unfortunately, the Cummins engine and hydraulically operated gearbox proved very noisy for coach operation.

Following the takeover by Blackpool Transport Services Limited as described on page 56, a number of double-deckers were transferred to Fylde. Among them was Blackpool No. 364 which had coach seating and it received Seagull livery and was numbered 47. In 1995 three Plaxton-bodied Leyland Tiger coaches were purchased from Timeline Travel Limited, having previously been new to Shearings, and they received fleet Nos. 21-23. They received Seagull livery in 1996.

XRN 36R was originally a Duple-bodied Leyland Leopard and carried fleet No. 36. It was rebodied by Duple in March 1989 and was carrying fleet No. 28 and Seagull fleetnames when photographed at the depot in May 1989. *(RM)*

A long way from home, and a passenger's view of the snow-lined streets as coach number 27 enters Warsaw as described in the text. *(MS)*

Immaculately turned out Van Hool-bodied DAF coach No. 26 is shown at North Shore, Blackpool, attending the Ribble Enthusiasts Club Annual Rally in August 1992 when only 4 months old and carrying the original white livery. This popular body design was seen in fleets throughout the country on a variety of chassis. *(MB)*

On the takeover by Blackpool Transport, one of the vehicles transferred was Blackpool 364, B364 UBV, a Leyland Atlantean with coach-seated East Lancashire body. It received fleet No. 47 and Seagull Coaches fleetnames and is shown passing through Lancaster on a Private Hire in August 1995. *(RM)*

Below is a wonderfully nostalgic reminder of Seagull in days long-gone-by as a Leyland Tiger waits for the photographer before running down the promenade. In the background one of Lytham's venerable open-top trams makes yet another journey back home. The tower looks on impassively. *(STA/BCVM)*

10 – Return of the Lion

In 1988 Memory Lane Coaches of Golbourne offered to Fylde Transport the opportunity to purchase an ex-Lytham St Annes Corporation Leyland Lion LT5c No. 34 which had been new in 1934 and carried Leyland bodywork. The sale was agreed and the Lion, with its radiator and other components stored in the saloon, was towed to Blue Buses where the front axle and brakes were overhauled and a new stainless steel exhaust obtained. Surprisingly, the steering ball pillars and dies, the brake clevis pins and bushes were all available in the stores as they were still used on modern vehicles. Also, the hydraulic brake seals were available from suppliers.

The torque converter gearbox was designed to give a maximum six to one ratio in torque converter drive and a direct drive 'top' gear. Designed in the UK the Lysholm Smith patented unit was a method of simplifying gear changing when retraining tram drivers to drive buses. Using lubricant made up of one part engine oil to five parts paraffin caused two major problems. Firstly, in hilly areas or in hot weather conditions, the paraffin would evaporate causing slip with loss of headway, this effect being compounded if the bus was driven further. Secondly, to regain headway a fitter was required to attend to top up the mixture and bleed out the air. Even with limited use as a preserved vehicle No. 34 suffered this problem and to improve matters, Blue Buses switched to Dextron 2, a modern automatic transmission fluid.

The structure of the Leyland bodywork was excellent. The roof was steel panelled and had become pock marked from standing out in the rain. To save repanelling many coats of undercoat were applied and well flatted between coats until a smooth finish was obtained. The prewar livery was matched to a tramway sign loaned to Masons Paints and the paintwork was finished using transfers of Coats of Arms still available from stock. Missing from the saloon were the art deco glass 'flower vase' light fittings originally fitted to the window pillars. A search in the cold store produced enough period light fittings which, when fitted into the roof above the windows were in character. The missing 'Gearless Bus' radiator badge was kindly donated and a gifted employee filed out the letters to make the word 'Leyland' which had been missing from the clutch cover.

Following the recovering of the seats in original patterned moquette all was ready for the launch. However, suspicious piles of sawdust were discovered revealing that woodworm had infested one of the seats. This was removed and a new one made. Finally, the Lion was ready to make its public debut at the Heart of the Pennines Rally at Halifax.

Number 34, the preserved 1936 Leyland Lion LT7c with Leyland bodywork, is shown with a full load of enthusiasts climbing out of the car park at Halifax in May 1992 with Mike Sagrott, Engineering Director, at the wheel. *(RM)*

When Fylde Transport Limited was taken over by Blackpool Transport Services Limited, the Lion was included in the deal and continues to be well cared for.

A further similar Leyland Lion numbered 44 is also still in existence. Over the years it has appeared at rallies but its condition has deteriorated and it is at present awaiting restoration.

Two more views of the preserved Lion, firstly at the 1992 Heart of the Pennines Rally and showing the distinctive rear colour scheme, wide centre pillar and rear indicator arrangement. Below is a more recent view, taken at Heaton Park Manchester at the Trans-Lancs Rally. The header tank for the torque-converter, always the identifying feature of buses with this transmission, is clearly visible on the bulkhead. The vehicle is absolutely pristine. *(JAS both)*

11 – Diversification

From the establishment of the limited company, it had been intended to take into the workshops repair work from other companies on a commercial basis. Due to the increase in fleet size, this was never achieved on the scale anticipated but there was one notable project which was undertaken. An AEC Regent 3 fleet No. 277 owned by Halifax Joint Omnibus Committee, was taken in for renovation to class 6 standard to enable it to operate as a Public Service Vehicle. Although the engine and chassis were in good order, much work was needed on the interior. The first job was to tie in the platform and stairs with the rear bulkhead riser. A new riser had been fitted sometime earlier but the platform and staircase had not been bolted to it, allowing the rear end to swing from side to side. Both saloons were fitted with new lino and the inner side panels recovered with brown Rexine. Houldsworths of Halifax were persuaded to produce new seating moquette in the correct style and the correct colours which were dyed specially.

After much searching a CAV spot lamp, now obsolete, was obtained brand new in a dust laden box and with this the project was complete.

The finished result, and Halifax Regent III makes a big impression at the Heart of the Pennines Rally, paint gleaming and looking as though it had just left the Park Royal factory. *(JAS)*

12 – Bus Fleet Improvements

To enable continued success it was necessary to update what was becoming an ageing fleet. Blackpool was having success with a fleet of Optare Delta-bodied DAF SB220 saloons and it was decided to purchase three of these from Optare in Leeds. They entered service in 1991 as numbers 1-3 and registered H1 - H3 FBT. They made a major impact on services 11/11A and were so good that they only entered the depot on servicing days and did not suffer any major failures during their time with Fylde.

A second and less costly way of improving the vehicles on routes 11/11A was to arrange for Northern Counties to refurbish and modernise five Leyland Atlanteans. The vehicles were numbers 84 - 88 dating from 1976/77. They were given complete new fronts, new cab heaters and demisters, new floor and seat coverings and cord trim to seat backs and ceilings. On completion they became numbers 71 - 75 and were provided with Irish registrations. Before being sent to Northern Counties the chassis received attention in the workshop and this included the fitting of front mounted radiators to three of them to improve reliability and the fitting of power-assisted steering gear removed from ex-Manchester Atlanteans. There were now eight smartly turned out vehicles supporting the 11/11A services.

Next came the biggest challenge of all. Hull City Transport had previously purchased five 33ft long Leyland Atlanteans with Alexander bodies from Bradford City Transport. Now withdrawn, they were offered for sale by Hull and four came to Fylde in an unusual way, the fifth having passed to a police crime prevention unit. By arrangement with a Barnsley dealer, the four were collected from Hull and taken to the Barnsley yard where the bodies were removed leaving just the lower saloon floor onto which the seat frames were placed before they were towed to Squires Gate depot. In return for the free collection and delivery service, the old Alexander bodies were given as payment. After some time in store, the chassis were taken in turn into the workshop to be reconditioned. Using spare Atlantean outriggers, the chassis were extended at the front by about 20 inches and following trials with Nos. 71-75, front mounted radiators were fitted. Cooling was provided using a Bristol RE electric motor and fan. After removal of the mechanical handbrake, spring brake units were fitted. Following the fitting of the overhauled engine and gearbox the exhaust was connected via a Leyland Leopard

One of the three DAF Deltas at the depot in May 1991 prior to the fitting of the destination blind. *(RM)*

silencer fitted across the very rear of the chassis adding another 14 inches to the length of the finished bus. Northern Counties added a stylish 'Paladin' single-deck body turning these old Bradford Leyland Atlanteans into modern buses ready to add further quality to the 11/11A main line services. There were now twelve good sound and reliable vehicles available.

However, doubts soon began to appear after Nos. 4 to 7 entered service as the vehicles seated only 42 and they were therefore unable to cope on service 11/11A which was becoming a victim of its own success. Hindsight clearly showed that they should have been rebodied as double-deckers. Following withdrawal of the Bristol REs,

mainly due to unreliability of the fluid flywheel seals and the non availability of steering box parts, numbers 4-7 took over operation on the 193 service previously operated by the Bristols.

Below: Bus No. 71 at Blackpool Airport after rebuilding and refurbishment by Northern Counties. *(MM)*

Bottom: After Northern Counties were taken over by Plaxtons, official photography became a side issue – this view of the new single-deck body on No. 7 was taken on an overbridge on the M55 *en route* back to Fylde. *(MS)*

13 – Support Services

As the fleet size increased between 1986 and 1990, improvements became necessary to ensure continued efficient operation. In the east shed, a second fuel pump was added to speed up fuelling and for continued operation should one pump fail. Beyond the pumps, the bus wash was re-sited giving a north - south servicing lane replacing the drive in, reverse out wash arrangement located in the centre shed. Extra parking outside was provided by taking up topsoil used many years previously for allotments and flower beds. This area was then covered with spent railway ballast supplied on eight wheel lorries at £30 per load.

Inside the building thick polythene sheeting was hung to create a wall between the west shed and the middle shed. The west shed became a new workshop area provided with transportable vehicle lifts, new gas heaters, new lighting, benches and electrical services. Just prior to the purchase by Blackpool Transport Services Limited, plans had been in place to re-locate the stores and to move the paint shop to improve accessibility and efficiency.

Whilst Blue Buses ended its life with quite an up to date servicing and workshop facility, it is worth noting that when the depot was dismantled the tramway track fan was still in place and trolley head wheels were still fixed to the wall where they had carried ropes to operate the wartime roof blackout.

Ex-Clyde Coast Services Northern Counties-bodied Leyland Atlantean, TSD 571S carried fleet No.171 when photographed at the depot on 19th August 1990 in the two shades of blue livery and carrying a bold advert to promote Blue Buses. *(RM)*

14 – Fylde Transport Ltd

The final chapter in the story is a short one. The Conservative government was encouraging local authorities to sell their transport undertakings and the management at Fylde secured single bidder status and Fylde Borough Transport Limited was sold to them in January 1994.

No great changes ensued but the arrangement was short lived for in May 1994 the business was sold to Blackpool Transport Services Limited which meant that the business passed back into municipal control, which was of course against government aspirations. It also meant that after many attempts Blackpool Council gained control of bus operations in Lytham St Annes.

A process of integration began and major changes in services took place in November 1994 to avoid duplication. Fylde's identity began to be absorbed into the parent company and whilst the 'Seagull Coaches' operation retained the two tone blue livery the buses were rebranded 'Blackpool and Fylde Blue Buses' and began to appear in a new livery of blue and cream, applied in a similar way to the Blackpool green and cream.

A new logo appeared incorporating the Blackpool Tower and waves similar to that which had been used by Blackpool Transport since deregulation in 1986. A number of buses from the Blackpool fleet were transferred to Squires Gate depot and appeared in the blue and cream livery. Later, in 1996 the 'Blue Buses' identity was dropped and buses were then painted in the standard Blackpool livery of green and cream. The ex-Fylde vehicles were renumbered into the Blackpool fleet numbering system.

On 21st July 1996 Fylde's operating licence was surrendered in favour of an expanded licence for Blackpool Transport and it was announced that the former Fylde operation would be referred to as 'Squires Gate depot'. The depot continued in use until 12th April 1999 after which it was vacated and the allocation was transferred to Rigby Road depot in Blackpool.

The final end came in June 2001 when the depot was demolished and the site was subsequently developed for housing. This brought to a conclusion the history of a well admired operator. Fortunately, a number of vehicles have been preserved and these are illustrated in the photographic section of this publication.

Formerly No. 101 in the Blackpool fleet, and numerically the first Optare Delta in the fleet, G101 NBV was renumbered 8 when transferred to the Blue Bus fleet. It is seen entering Talbot Square, Blackpool in June 1995. *(RM)*

Facing page: Blackpool 323 was one of the vehicles transferred to the 'Blue Fleet' and it was photographed at Squires Gate in June 1995 heading for Lytham. *(RM)*

Below: Looking rather bland in the Blue Bus version of the Blackpool livery in August 1996 is No. 58, one of the first Atlanteans dating from 1970 and numbered 77 when it was new. *(MB)*

15 - A Pictorial Review

Gas tram No. 17 passes No. 14 on the loop line on Clifton Drive in St Annes with the Congregational Church on the right. *(SPC)*

A posed photograph of gas car No. 1 dating from 1896. *(JNC)*

On 21st May 1903, No. 5 became the first electric car to arrive in Lytham and seems to have created great interest. *(LHG)*

Tram No. 9 makes its way between the sandhills en route to Lytham. *(JNC)*

A scene on Lytham Road, Blackpool with Blackpool car No. 43 making its way south towards Lytham with another car heading towards Blackpool. *(LHG)*

Travelling along the road between the sand dunes, towards Blackpool is Car No. 18 dating from 1903. *(JNC)*

Tram No. 17 heads along Clifton Drive, South, towards Lytham with Fairhaven Methodist Church prominent on the right of the photograph. *(JNC)*

A posed photograph of Tram No. 15 with the crew looking smart and proud. Note the title on the rocker panel. *(JNC)*

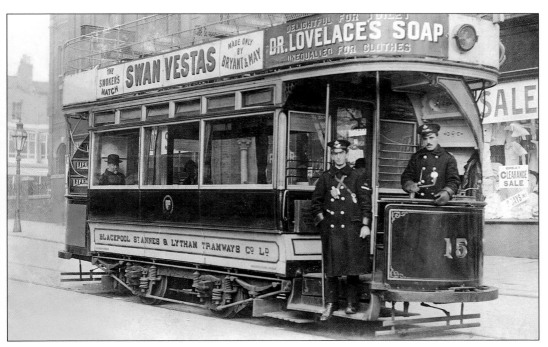

A young lady holds on to her hat, a regular necessity on the Fylde Coast, as Tram No. 20 trundles along. The ladies on the opposite side of the road appear to be looking with interest at this 'modern' form of transport. *(JNC)*

Cars 11 and 16 pass as they travel through the sandhills with No 11 heading for Blackpool and No. 16 for St Annes and Lytham. *(LHG)*

Trams 20 and 46 meet at the Woodlands Road stop on Clifton Drive South. The tram stop shelter is still maintained in good condition as a general shelter with seating. On the right of the photograph is Fairhaven Methodist Church *(JNC)*

Cars Nos. 1 and 15 pass as the former heads towards Lytham Hospital and the other to Blackpool Central Station. *(JNC)*

Tram No. 1 makes its way south along Clifton Drive towards Lytham with the spire of The Drive Methodist Church prominent in the background. *(LHG)*

A well loaded double-deck crossbench car is posed for the photographer with conductors on both lower and upper decks. *(LHG)*

Number 6 was photographed outside the depot following refurbishment in 1927. *(LHG)*

Car No. 4 displays the zig-zag livery as it departs from Gynn Square, Blackpool for St Annes. *(STA)*

One of the ex-Dearne single-deck cars numbered 51 - 54 is shown at Gynn Square, Blackpool. *(SPC)*

A scene at Gynn Square, Blackpool with a Blackpool railcoach following and contrasting with a Lytham car. *(SPC)*

The Mayor of Lytham St Annes, Alderman C F Critchley takes the controls of No. 41, the first of the Pullman Cars numbered 41-50 and delivered in 1924 These were the only new trams to be purchased by Lytham St Annes Corporation. *(JNC)*

One of the Pullman Cars numbered 41-50 and delivered in 1924 leaves Lytham Square for Gynn Square, Blackpool. The route board covers the fleet number, a practice which was common in Lytham St Annes. *(STA)*

Former Preston Corporation car No. 56 awaits departure from Lytham Square. *(STA)*

Four cars numbered 51-54 were purchased from Dearne District Light Railways in 1933. They were new in 1924 and Lytham St Annes paid £500 for the four. No 51 is shown here at North Pier. *(JNC)*

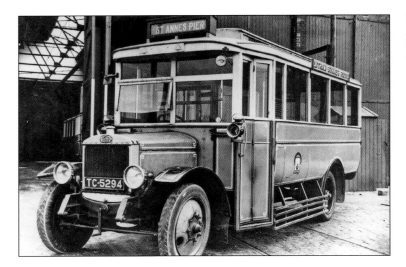

Number 3, a Guy B type with Blackburn Aero body, dating from 1923 is shown at the depot. *(RMC)*

A vehicle thought to be No. 12, a Guy B type with Guy body dating from 1926, is shown on Clifton Drive with an unidentified vehicle travelling in the opposite direction. *(JNC)*

A Guy J type with Guy 'toastrack' body was purchased in 1925 and was designated a 'runabout'. Accordingly, it received fleet No. R1. *(RMC)*

One person operation, early thirties style, as a passenger pays his fare on boarding one of the early normal control buses. *(JNC)*

A passenger alights in St Annes Square from one of the 1923 Blackburn Aero-bodied Guy B type single-deckers. *(JNC)*

Number 6, a Guy B type with Blackburn Aero body, the last of the first six motor buses supplied in 1923, is shown in a rural setting. *(JNC)*

An early scene from St Annes Square with two unidentified motor buses, one having just crossed the railway bridge towards the Square and the other heading away from the Square. Cycles abound. *(JNC)*

Posed for the photographer, at the entrance to Ashton Gardens when new, is No. 8 one of the two Burlingham-bodied Leyland KP2 models delivered in 1933 and numbered 2 and 8. *(STA)*

In 1935 four Leyland LC1 models were purchased from Burnley, Colne and Nelson Joint Omnibus Committee and were fitted with new Burlingham open-top bodies in 1938 and 1939. No. 25 is shown when new. *(JNC)*

1934 Leyland Lion LT5A No. 24 is illustrated with open-top single-deckers at St Annes Pier. *(JNC)*

Above: Number 31 was one of the 1935 Burlingham-bodied Leyland LT7c models rebuilt by Blackpool Coachcraft to open-top arrangement in 1946. The 'Gearless Bus' sign on the radiator is clearly visible in this view. *(RMC)*

Below and facing page foot: Number 33, a Leyland-bodied Leyland LT7c dating from 1936, stands in St Annes Square awaiting departure to Lytham Square on service 4 in the postwar period. *(KS)*

The driver and conductor chat while awaiting departure time from Lytham Square to Blackpool with 1937 Leyland TD4c No. 46, the full-fronted body and torque-converter being decidedly outdated by now. *(KS)*

In May 1952, wartime Daimler CWA6 with Duple body was awaiting departure from Lytham to Blackpool on service 11. *(RM)*

Photographed in Blackpool, in postwar days, outside the original Marks and Spencer store is 1936 Leyland-bodied Leyland TD4c No. 38 with No. 11, a 1948 Leyland-bodied PD2, behind. *(RM)*

Number 49 was numerically the last of the Leyland TD4c models to be purchased in 1937, the remaining 1937 double-deckers Nos. 50 to 53 being to the later TD5c specification. *(JNC)*

1937 Leyland TD4c No. 49 was converted to open-top together with sister vehicle No. 46 in 1960 but had a short life in this form, being withdrawn in 1961 *(JNC)*

Postwar Fleet Renewal

Leyland-bodied Leyland PD1 No. 16 from the first batch of postwar buses delivered in 1946 was photographed when new by Leyland Motors. *(JNC)*

1946 Leyland PD1 No. 20 is shown in Lytham about to depart to Blackpool on service 11 on 24th May 1952. *(RM)*

Lytham St Annes was an early user of the Leyland PD2, the first examples being purchased in 1948 numbered 10 to 15 and fitted with Leyland bodies. No. 13 is shown leaving Lytham Square for Ansdell and St Annes in July 1970. No. 15 from this batch had a short life, being withdrawn in 1958 following a collision with a tramcar. *(BD)*

Number 14 from the 1948 batch of Leyland PD2/1s emerges from St George's Road, St Annes into Clifton Drive in July 1972 en route to Blackpool Airport. *(BD)*

Leyland PD2/12 No. 5 taken in St Annes in July 1972 shows the final style of double-deck body produced by Leyland prior to the cessation of bus body building in 1953. No. 5 was the first of a batch numbered 5 to 9 delivered in 1951. No 7 was withdrawn in December 1969 following an accident but the others survived and were transferred to Fylde Borough Transport in April 1974. An offside view of No. 8 is shown below, also in St Annes. *(BD)*

The first postwar single-deckers arrived in 1957 in the form of three Leyland PSUC1/1 with locally built Burlingham bodies. The upper photograph taken in St Annes in October 1960 and the lower photograph taken in St Annes in October 1964 display the characteristic lines of the Burlingham service bus body of that time with the large radius to the window pans evident. *(RM)*

A surprise acquisition in 1959 was a single front-engined single-decker purchased from Lancaster City Transport to whom it had been new in March 1947. The chassis was a Leyland PS1 and the body was by Crossley Motors. It is shown parked outside the depot. *(RM/RLW)*

With the cessation of bus body building at Leyland in 1953, Lytham St Annes had to look elsewhere for bodies for the five Leyland PD2s which were purchased in 1957. The order went to Northern Counties Motor and Engineering Company of Wigan who supplied well proportioned four-bay bodies as illustrated by No. 57 as it leaves Lytham Square for Blackpool in July 1970. This was the first time that the undertaking had purchased double-deck bodies from other than Leyland Motors, apart from the two wartime Daimlers allocated to them by the Ministry of War Transport in 1943. *(BD)*

Shown in St Annes in August 1973 is Northern Counties-bodied Leyland PD2 No. 58 showing the Lytham St Annes fleetname which it would lose seven months later with the transfer to Fylde Borough Council. *(BD)*

In 1962, two Leyland PD1 double-deckers were purchased from Warrington Corporation Transport and numbered 23 and 24. They had Alexander bodies built to the Leyland design and were new in November 1946. This was at a time when there was pressure on the Leyland bodyshops and a number of operators received bodies built by Alexander to the Leyland design. Note the service number display in its own box under the canopy. *(HPC)*

In July 1970 a Leyland PD2 with MCW body was acquired from Blackpool Corporation Transport Department. The full-fronted body design brought back memories of prewar Lytham St Annes double-deckers which featured this design. It was numbered 74 and is shown heading towards St Annes Square in June 1974. *(BD)*

Two photographs showing the effect of the livery change on the MCW-bodied Leyland PD2s delivered in 1960. The upper photograph shows No. 62 in St Annes Square in July 1972 carrying the original livery. The lower photograph, also taken in St Annes Square 13 months later, shows No. 67 in the new livery, with its extensive area of unrelieved white between decks, which did nothing to alleviate the ungainly proportions of this body design. The fact that the vehicle is carrying the Lytham St Annes fleetname confirms that the livery change commenced before the transfer of the undertaking to Fylde Borough Council. *(BD)*

1964 Massey-bodied Leyland PD2 No. 70 is shown passing the depot in Squires Gate Lane on a quiet Sunday afternoon in September 1972. *(BD)*

Massey-bodied Leyland PD2 No. 70 shows the new livery as it enters St Annes Square in April 1980 with the United Reformed Church in the background. *(RM)*

Rear-Engined Single-Deckers

The year 1969 saw the arrival of three rear-engined single-deckers, the first in the fleet and comprising Leyland Panther chassis with Northern Counties bodies. They were numbered 71 to 73 and No. 72 is shown at St Annes Square operating on service 4 in July 1970. *(BD)*

Contrasting livery styles on the Leyland Panther single-deckers are shown by No. 72 in the upper photograph in the original livery whilst the lower photograph shows No. 73 in the later livery and approaching St Annes Square on service 3 in August 1973. *(BD)*

The Bristol RE was generally regarded as the most successful of the rear-engined single-deckers but initially it was only available to nationalised companies in the Tilling and Scottish Bus Groups In an attempt to provide a similar model with Gardner engine to other operators, Seddon introduced its RU model. Crosville Motor Service had 100 Seddon RU imposed on them by National Bus Company and the problems encountered are well documented elsewhere. Lytham St Annes took delivery of six Seddon RU models with bodies by Seddon's associated company, Pennine Coachcraft, in 1972 and one of these, No. 50 was photographed in St Annes in August 1973. They were the last new vehicles to be supplied to Lytham St Annes Corporation Transport and all passed to Fylde Borough Transport. All were withdrawn by June 1982. *(BD)*

Pennine-bodied Seddon RU No. 47 is shown at St Annes Square in July 1976 carrying the later Fylde livery with yellow band and the Fylde Borough fleetname with coat of arms. *(BD)*

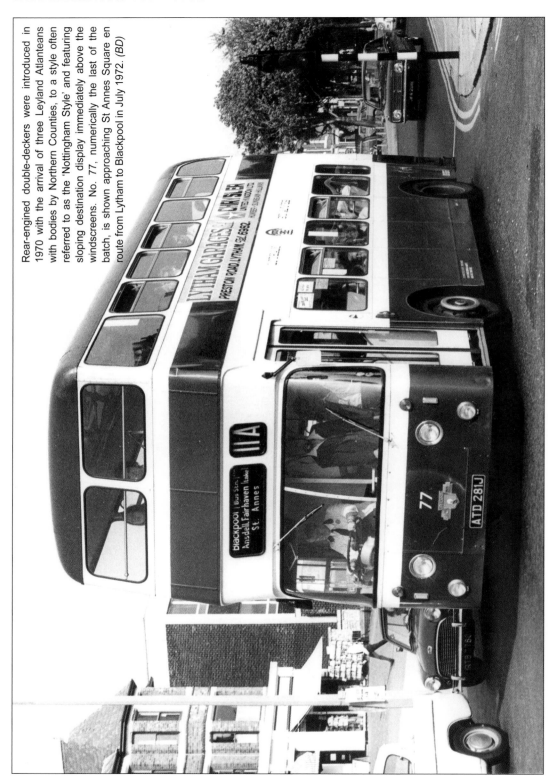

Rear-engined double-deckers were introduced in 1970 with the arrival of three Leyland Atlanteans with bodies by Northern Counties, to a style often referred to as the 'Nottingham Style' and featuring sloping destination display immediately above the windscreens. No. 77, numerically the last of the batch, is shown approaching St Annes Square en route from Lytham to Blackpool in July 1972. (BD)

On 29th June 1974 Leyland PD2 No. 5 is shown in St Annes carrying the Fylde fleetname. *(BD)*

Number 60, one of the 1957 Leyland PD2s with Northern Counties bodies had been repainted into the latest livery with yellow band when photographed in St Annes Square in July 1976 and carried the Fylde Borough name with coat of arms. *(BD)*

The Coach Era begins

Plaxton-bodied Leyland Leopard coach No. 44 leaves Blackpool Coliseum Coach Station on 20th August 1977 duplicating the 08.40 hours departure on service 281 to Bradford operating on hire to National Express. *(BD)*

Purchased at the same time as No. 44 in 1975 was No. 43. The coaches were used on local services as well as Private Hire and Express work. Number 43 is shown in St Annes Square operating local service 1 in July 1976. *(BD)*

Photographed parked at Keswick coach park whilst on an excursion duty is Duple-bodied Leyland Leopard No 36. *(JNC/GC)*

Fylde drivers, Donovan and Ellis proudly hold the Yeates cup presented at the Blackpool Coach Rally in April 1978 for the best coach supplied by Yeates. It had been presented by Councillor Parkinson, Chairman of Blackpool Transport Committee. *(JNC)*

Bristol RE No. 38 was carrying an overall advert for the 'Blue Bus Rambler' ticket when photographed in Talbot Road, Blackpool in September 1988. *(RM)*

Photographed leaving St Annes Square for Wesham in September 1985 is Bristol RE No. 41 advertising the Lancashire County Council Senior Citizens Half Fare Travel Concession. *(MB)*

Burnley, Colne and Nelson Leyland National 1 No. 135 is shown on loan to Lytham St Annes Corporation with Blackpool MCW-bodied Leyland PD3 number 526 behind. Further Leyland Nationals were operated on loan but no orders were placed for this vehicle. *(JNC)*

On 25th June 1977 Leyland Atlantean No. 80 travels along Lytham Road, Blackpool on service 11A to Lytham Square. *(BD)*

Lytham Road, Blackpool provides the setting for this view of Leyland Atlantean No. 83 as it heads towards St Annes and Lytham Square on 4th June 1977. In the background, having just left Coliseum Coach Station is a Bristol RE with ECW body in the National Bus Company dual-purpose livery. *(BD)*

Number 76 waits at Coliseum Coach Station, Blackpool on 3rd August 1974 before duplicating the 10.00 hours departure to Manchester. *(BD)*

Willowbrook-bodied Leyland Atlantean No. 82 far from home, arriving in Manchester on hire to Ribble Motor Services and duplicating the 10.00 hours departure from Blackpool on the well known X60 service on Saturday 16th August 1975 when only 5 months old. Behind is Ribble Leyland Leopard No. 665 in the drab all over poppy red NBC livery arriving on the X50 service from Morecambe. Note that the Fylde vehicle was displaying 'Manchester' on its destination blind and 'On Hire to Ribble Motor Services Ltd.' in the via blind thus eliminating the need to use untidy window stickers in a situation such as this. *(BD)*

The purchase of the first double-deckers by Fylde Borough Transport was a complicated affair as explained in the text. The order materialised in 1975 as six Leyland Atlanteans with Willowbrook bodies on Northern Counties frames. They were numbered 78 to 83 and No. 82 is illustrated here on Central Drive, Blackpool on Saturday 9th August 1975 heading for Lytham. In the background is a Blackpool Transport Leyland PD3 with MCW bodywork. *(BD)*

Pre-Used Vehicles

In 1977 six Leyland Atlanteans with Metro Cammell Weymann bodies designed to meet the requirements of Liverpool City Transport were purchased from Merseyside PTE. Only five entered service and No. 89 was photographed having just passed under the recently demolished bridge on Central Promenade, Blackpool in April 1980. *(RM)*

Further Roe-bodied Leyland Atlanteans were purchased from Hull City Transport in 1987 and were numbered 121 to 128, 45, 46 and 76. The latter is shown entering Talbot Square, Blackpool in July 1987. The centre door has been panelled over in a rather crude way, no doubt because of the necessity to place the vehicle in service as soon as possible. *(RM)*

In the unmistakable surroundings of Blackpool Central Promenade, No. 91 one of the ex-Hull City Transport Atlanteans, heads south, followed by one of Blackpool Transport's Routemasters in October 1987. *(RM)*

Ex-Greater Manchester Leyland Atlantean with Northern Counties bodywork, Fylde No. 164 in the two shades of blue livery travels down Talbot Road, Blackpool heading for Lytham in May 1989. Fylde had great faith in the eyesight of its potential passengers, judging by the amount of information displayed on the single line destination display. *(RM)*

Arrival of the Minis

Engineering Director, Mike Sagrott stand proudly by minibuses 104 and 105 shortly after delivery. *(MSC)*

With a clear blue winter sky overhead, in March 1989, minibus No. 142, one of five purchased in November 1988, heads through Blackpool on service 55. *(HP)*

Minibus No. 102 advertises the 'Beachcomber' 7-Day Ticket as it heads south on Blackpool Promenade in June 1987. *(HP)*

In the days of Blackpool ownership in August 1996, minibus No. 105 still retained the two shades of blue livery when photographed in Cleveleys. *(MB)*

In two shades of blue livery and carrying lettering for the Promenade Service, No. 59, an ex-Hull Atlantean, is shown outside the depot in May 1991. *(RM)*

In overall advert livery for the Granada Studios Tour operated by Seagull Coaches, ex-Hull Atlantean No. 52 operates on the No. 1 Promenade Service in Blackpool and stops for passengers at the Tower in August 1993. *(RM)*

In addition to vehicles acquired from Hull City Transport, three Daimler Fleetlines were purchased from Grimsby Cleethorpes Transport in 1987. They had similar Roe bodies to the ex-Hull Atlanteans but were found to be in better condition. They were numbered 47 to 49 and No. 47 was photographed passing the Norbreck Castle Hotel, heading south on Queens Promenade, Blackpool, in July 1987. *(RM)*

TSD 571S was one of two Leyland Atlanteans acquired from Clyde Coast Services, Ardrossan in February 1990, the other being MSD 141P. When acquired they were numbered 170 (MSD 141P) and 171. Number 171 was renumbered 71 in April 1991 and again renumbered to 70 in July 1991. Fylde had a habit of renumbering vehicles. It is shown passing North Pier, Blackpool in June 1994. Note that it is carrying the type of destination display fitted to the ex-Greater Manchester Atlanteans. *(RM)*

Seagull Coaches

Ex-Seagull Leyland Leopard No. 30 at the depot in March 1989 after painting in the blue livery and application of the Seagull symbol and fleetname. *(RM)*

Duple Laser-bodied Leyland Tiger, No. 27, new in 1987 is shown at the depot in May 1989 carrying Seagull fleetnames. *(RM)*

NJI 5505 carrying fleet No. 45 had coach seating and Seagull fleetnames applied. It was photographed in Blackpool in August 1993 showing Manchester as the destination, possibly on the Granada Studios Tour. *(RM)*

G813 RNC was new to Shearings in 1990 and purchased by Fylde in May 1993 along with sister vehicle G812 RNC. It was photographed in Blackpool in August 1993 carrying Seagull Coaches fleetname. *(RM)*

Number 1 was one of three Optare Delta models purchased in 1991 and is shown in Talbot Road, Blackpool in May 1993 passing Rumours Nightclub and with Sacred Heart Roman Catholic Church in the background. *(RM)*

Rebodied Leyland Atlantean No. 6, one of four provided with new Northern Counties single-deck bodies, is shown picking up passengers at Blackpool Tower in August 1993 en route to Lytham. *(RM)*

Northern Counties-bodied Atlantean No. 71 is shown passing the junction of Talbot Road and Abingdon Street in Blackpool in May 1993 with a Blackpool East Lancashire-bodied Atlantean in the background. *(RM)*

A front nearside view of one of the bodies under construction at the works of Northern Counties prior to the fitting of external panels. *(MS)*

With external panels fitted, work continues on one of the bodies at Northern Counties. *(MS)*

A nearside rear view of No. 7 taken en route from the Northern Counties works to Fylde. (MS)

Number 24, a Leyland-bodied Leyland LT5A dating from 1934 and acquired by Lytham St Annes in 1935 is now preserved and was photographed at Leyland on 8th July 2007. *(BD)*

Number 34, a 1936 Leyland-bodied Leyland LT7c, is preserved and is shown at Fleetwood Tram Sunday on 21st July 2002. It retains its torque convertor transmission. *(BD)*

Photographed entering Salford University in August 1971, at the start of the Trans Pennine Run, is preserved Lytham St Annes Leyland LT7c with Leyland body, No. 44 which was new in 1937. It still exists in 2009. *(HP)*

Preserved No. 19 a Leyland-bodied Leyland PD1, was one of the batch of six similar vehicles which formed the first postwar deliveries to Lytham St Annes. It is shown on a special service at Bispham on 10th June 2006. *(BD)*

Photographed on Middle Walk, Blackpool, when taking part in the Ribble Enthusiasts Club, Southport to Blackpool run in August 2000 is preserved No. 70 a Leyland PD2 with Massey body dating from 1964. *(HP)*

Number 77 photographed on Lytham Road, Blackpool on 27th June 1981 shows the revised position for the destination indicator, as it crosses the tram rails. *(BD)*

Northern Counties-bodied Leyland Panther rear engined single-decker No.73 was one of three supplied in 1969 with a further three following in 1970. It is shown at Lytham in February 1981. *(MB)*

Photographed in Blackpool in June 1980 heading for Lytham, Saltcoates Road, on service 31A is Pennine bodied Seddon RU No. 46. *(MB)*

Plaxton-bodied Leyland Leopard coach No. 42 in blue and yellow livery is shown at Ashfield Road, Bispham in September 1987 on local service work. *(MB)*

Leaving Lytham Square for St Annes on service 193 from Wesham in August 1985 is Bristol RE No. 40. *(HP)*

Atlantean No. 87 moves away from St Annes Square in July 1987 operating service 11C to Blackpool via Queensway. In pre-deregulation days, service 11C, although a joint service with Blackpool, was operated by Blackpool vehicles. *(HP)*

Travelling south on Central Promenade, Blackpool in August 1983, is Atlantean No. 88 operating on service 11A. *(HP)*

Snow is something of a rarity on the Fylde Coast but it snowed in February 1978 and this is evident in this photograph of No. 94 at Squires Gate. It was one of six Atlanteans with MCW bodies designed to the requirement of Liverpool City Transport, purchased by Fylde in 1977 from Merseyside PTE. Only five entered service with Fylde, the other being used for spares. *(MB)*

Number 36, a Leyland Leopard with Duple coach body, went on long term hire to Southend Corporation Transport when that operator was running express services to London. It was photographed at Hyde Park Corner in April 1984. *(HP)*

Having just left St Annes Square No. 92 climbs over the railway bridge as it heads to Lytham on service 11 in June 1987. *(HP)*

When is a Blue Bus not blue? When it has been recently purchased from Grimsby Cleethorpes Transport and has been pressed into service prior to repainting. No. 49 shown at Clifton Drive, St Annes in July 1987, was one of three Daimler Fleetlines with Roe bodies purchased in April 1987 and numbered 47 to 49. Although they had the same type of Roe body as the Atlanteans from Hull, they were said to be in better condition with less framework corrosion. *(HP)*

The late Ken Martin stands at the front of another Atlantean, TKH 276H at the motorway services on the M62 on delivery from Hull. Comparison with the photograph below shows the similarity between the Hull and Fylde liveries. *(MS)*

Photographed leaving St Annes Square for Blackpool in June 1987 is Atlantean No. 84 dating from 1976. It was operating via the 'back route' numbered 11C. Prior to deregulation this service, although a joint service, had always been operated by Blackpool vehicles. *(HP)*

Ex-Hull Atlantean No. 131 had just emerged from Blackpool's Talbot Road Bus Station en route to Lytham when photographed in April 1989. *(HP)*

Number 43 had just departed from Cleveleys Bus Station for Lytham when photographed in May 1994. This vehicle was originally No. 99 and was renumbered 43 in March 1992. It was refurbished and rebuilt with a Paladin-style front by Northern Counties in August 1992. *(HP)*

The new roof, made by a local joiner, is tried for size on Atlantean No. 89. *(MS)*

Operating on contract to Lancashire County Council, No. 64, an ex-Greater Manchester Atlantean, leaves Preston Bus Station for Blackpool on service 158 on Sunday 15th September 1991 with a Fishwick Leyland National on the stand awaiting departure. *(BD)*

Ex-Greater Manchester Atlantean No. 169 turns out of St Annes Square operating the 16.15 hours journey on service 193 from Spring Gardens to Wesham on Saturday 29th July 1989 followed by Blackpool Routemaster No. 533 on service 12 to Blackpool. *(BD)*

Minibus No. 122 turns out of Nutter Road into Victoria Road, Cleveleys in August 1994 in the days before Victoria Road was made one way at this point. *(MB)*

B364 UBV, a coach-seated East Lancashire Coachbuilders-bodied Leyland Atlantean, was originally No. 364 in the Blackpool fleet. On passing to Fylde it received Seagull Coaches livery and fleet No. 47. It is shown at Fleetwood on an excursion on 22nd August 1995. No doubt its passengers would have been to the famous Fleetwood Market. *(BD)*

This Leyland Leopard was originally No. 36 and was renumbered 28 when it received this new Duple body in March 1989 It was reregistered TRN 772 when it re-entered service in June 1989. It is shown at Windermere on 12th August 1990. *(BD)*

Number 1, an Optare Delta, one of three purchased in 1991, is shown at Squires Gate in August 1994 heading for Lytham Square on service 11A. *(MB)*

Rebodied Leyland Atlantean No. 6 is shown parked in Cleveleys Bus Station in August 1994. It was one of four Leyland Atlanteans rebodied as single-deckers by Northern Counties in 1993. Originally the chassis were new with Alexander bodies to Bradford City Transport, passing to West Yorkshire PTE and then to Hull City Transport before purchase by Fylde. *(MB)*

Contrasting livery styles are shown in this photograph taken at Blackpool Tower in August 1996. In the foreground is Atlantean No. 81 showing the Blue Bus version of the Blackpool livery whilst at the rear No. 43 still displays the two shades of blue livery. *(RM)*

Ex-Blackpool Transport East Lancashire-bodied Leyland Atlantean No. 322 is shown at Cleveleys in October 1995 in the Blue Buses version of the Blackpool livery. *(MB)*

The Blackpool Style livery was short-lived because the operator adopted colour coded liveries for different routes, three of which serving Lytham St Annes are shown here.

Entering St Annes Square in July 2002 Blackpool No. 303 an East Lancashire-bodied Dennis Trident displays the dark green and yellow livery for service 14. *(HP)*

Crossing Victoria Square, Cleveleys, with the destination blind already set for the return journey to St Annes Square, Blackpool No. 322 shows the turquoise and yellow livery for service 11. *(HP)*

Showing the purple and yellow livery for service 7 is Blackpool Optare Delta No. 126 at St Annes Square in winter sunshine on 18th February 2002. *(HP)*

APPENDIX 1 TRAM FLEET SUMMARY

Gas Trams

YEAR IN SERVICE	FLEET Nos	ENGINE		SEATS	BUILDER
1896	1-4	Otto 15HP Twin Cylinder		24/16	Ashbury Railway Carriage and Iron Co.
1897	5-20	Otto 15HP Twin Cylinder		30/22	Lancaster Carriage & Wagon Co.

Electric Trams

YEAR IN SERVICE	FLEET Nos.	DETAILS	BOGIE	BODY	SEATS	NOTES
1903	1-20	Open Top	BEC SB60	BEC	22/32	1, 3
1903	21-30	Open Top	BEC SB60	BEC	22/32	2, 3
1905	31-40	Open Top Crossbench	Brush	Brush	34/34	3
1924	41-50	Balcony	Peckham	Eng.Elec.	23/38	
1933	51-54	Single Deck	Peckham	Eng.Elec.	36	Built 1924 ex Dearne District Light Railway.
1933	55	Enclosed	Brush	Brush	32/44?	Built 1915 Ex Accrington Corporation
1934	56	Enclosed	Preston Standard	Preston	22/40	Built 1928/9 ex Preston Corporation

Notes
1. Cars 6, 9, 11 reseated 20/32 in 1927/8. Car 6 remounted on Brush 21E truck.
2. Rebuilt by UEC in 1906 with crossbench lower deck seating to seat 28/32. No. 26 became sweeper / grinder in 1930.
3. Cars 1-40 were new to Blackpool, St Annes and Lytham Tramways Comany Limited passing to St Annes on the sea Urban District Council on 1st November 1920 and to Lytham St Annes Corporation Tramways on 9th November 1922.

APPENDIX 2 FLEET LIST SUMMARY

YEAR	REG.	FLEET Nos.	CHASSIS Nos.	BODY	SEATING	NOTES
LYTHAM ST ANNES CORPORATION						
1923	TC 4897-8	1,2	Guy B	Blackburn Aero	B20F	
1923	TC 5294	3	Guy B	Blackburn Aero	B20F	
1923	TC 5300	4	Guy B	Blackburn Aero	B20F	
1923	TC 5852	5	Guy B	Blackburn Aero	B20F	
1923	TC 5875	6	Guy B	Blackburn Aero	B20F	
1924	TC 8194-6	7-9	Guy B	Blackburn Aero	B20F	
1925	TD 2273	R1	Guy J	Guy	B20T	
1926	TD 6787-9	10-12	Guy B	Guy	B20F	
1931	TD 5925-6	14,15	Guy BB	Guy	B31F	New 5/26 to County, Lancaster passing to Ribble 1/29
1931	RF 1512	18	Guy BB	Guy	B20F	New 2/26 to Ripponden & Dist.
1931	WW1287	17	Guy BB	Guy	B20F	New 4/27 to Ripponden & Dist.
1931	UK 5266	16	Guy BB	Guy	B20F	New 5/28 to Ripponden & Dist.
1933	TJ 136-7	2,8	Leyland KP2	Burlingham	B20F	
1933	WU 450-1		Guy B	Guy	B20F	Ex Keighley West Yorks Not used by Lytham St.Annes
1933	WU 453		Guy B	Guy	B20F	do.
1933	WU 5320-1	20,21	Guy B	Guy	B20F	Ex Keighley West Yorks 21 entered service in 3/34
1933	TD 9146-7	23,22	Guy B	Guy	B26F	New 1927 to Burnley, Colne & Nelson
	CK 3966		Guy BB	Guy	B26F	New 1928 to Viking. Not used by Lytham St. Annes.
1935	ATC 729-31	29-31	Leyland LT7c	Burlingham	B34R	
1935	TJ 6760	24	Leyland LT5A	Leyland	B32R	Ex Demonstrator
1935	TD 8352-3	25,26	Leyland LC1	Leyland	B26F	25-28 New 1927 to
1935	TE 537	27	Leyland LC1	Leyland	B26F	Burnley, Colne &
1935	TE 1639	28	Leyland LC1	Leyland	B26F	Nelson
1936	ATE 734	32	Leyland LT7c	Burlingham	B34R	
1936	BTB 927-8	33,34	Leyland LT7c	Leyland	B34R	
1936	BTB 929-30	35,36	Leyland TD4c	Leyland	FH30/24R	
1936	BTC 621-3	37-39	Leyland TD4c	Leyland	FH30/24R	
1936	BTC 624	40	Leyland LT7c	Leyland	B34R	
1937	BTF 21-4	41-44	Leyland LT7c	Leyland	B34R	
1937	BTF 25-29	45-49	Leyland TD4c	Leyland	FH30/24R	
1937	CTC 27-30	50-53	Leyland TD5c	Leyland	FH30/24R	
1937	DK 4081	22	Leyland PLC1		C26F	Ex ES
1937	DK 5053	23	Leyland PLC1		C26F	do
1939	ETD 990	54	Leyland KPZ04	Burlingham	DP25R	
1940	FM 4303	21	Leyland PLSC1	Leyland	B31R	Ex CrMS
1943	FTD 617	22	Daimler CWA6	Duple	H30/26R	
1944	FTD 618	23	Daimler CWA6	Duple	H30/26R	
1946	GTB 903-5	19,17,18	Leyland PD1	Leyland	H30/26R	
1946	GTB 906-8	16,20,21	Leyland PD1	Leyland	H30/26R	
1948	JTD 381-6	10-15	Leyland PD2/1	Leyland	H30/26R	FBT.10,12,14
1951	NTD 574-8	5-9	Leyland PD2/12	Leyland	H30/26R	FBT 5,6,8,9
1957	367-9 BTJ	54-56	Leyland PSUC1/1	Burlingham	B44F	FBT
1957	765-60 CTD	57-61	Leyland PD2/20	NCME	H30/28R	FBT
1959	HTB 442	22	Leyland PS1	Crossley	B36R	Ex LCT
1960	45-50 NTD	62-67	Leyland PD2/30	MCCW	H35/28R	FBT
1962	EED 4-5	23,24	Leyland PD1	Alexander	H30/26R	Ex WCT
1964	CTF 625-7B	68-70	Leyland PD2A/27	Massey	H37/27F	FBT
1969	TTF 743-5H	71-73	Leyland PSUR1A/1R	NCME	B49D	FBT
1970	ATD 279-81J	75-77	Leyland PDR1A/1	NCME	H44/33F	FBT
1970	LFV 309	74	Leyland PD2/21	MCCW	FH35/24R	Ex BI FBT
1972	STJ 845-50L	45-50	Seddon RU 6LX	Pennine	B47D	FBT

APPENDIX 2 FLEET LIST SUMMARY

YEAR	REG.	FLEET Nos.	CHASSIS Nos	BODY	SEATING	NOTES

FYLDE BOROUGH TRANSPORT

YEAR	REG.	FLEET Nos.	CHASSIS Nos	BODY	SEATING	NOTES
1974	VTJ 443-4M	43-44	Leyland PSU3B/4R	Plaxton	C53F	
1975	HRN 97N	42	Leyland PSU3C/4R	Plaxton	C53F	
1975	HRN 98-103N	78-83	Leyland AN68/1R	NCME/W'brook	H43/31F	Note 1
1975	HRN 104-8N	37-41	Bristol RESL6L	ECW	DP44F	
1976	OCK 84P	84	Leyland AN68A/1R	NCME	H43/31F	
1977	XRN 36R	36	Leyland PSUC3/4R	Duple	C53F	
1977	EBV 85-8S	85-8	Leyland AN68A/1R	NCME	H43/31F	
1977	609 KD	89	Leyland PDR1/1	MCCW	H43/34F	Ex Mside
1977	633 KD	90	Leyland PDR1/1	MCCW	H43/34F	do
1977	637 KD	(91)	Leyland PDR1/1	MCCW	H43/34F	do
1977	646 KD	92	Leyland PDR1/1	MCCW	H43/34F	do
1977	667 KD	93	Leyland PDR1/1	MCCW	H43/34F	do
1977	699 KD	94	Leyland PDR1/1	MCCW	H43/34F	do
1978	OCK 35S	35	Leyland PSU3E/4	Duple	C53F	
1979	OHG 33-4T	33-4	Leyland PSU3E/4R	Duple	C53F	
1979	OHG 95T	95	Leyland AN68A/1R	NCME	H43/31F	
1979	ARN 808/10/16C	30-32	Leyland PSU3/3R	Weymann	DP49F	Ex RMS
1980	XHG 96V	96	Leyland AN68A/1R	NCME	H43/31F	
1980	XRN 28V	28	Volvo B58-56	Duple	C53F	
1980	XRN 29V	29	Leyland PSU3E/4R	Plaxton	C53F	
1981	HBV 97W	97	Leyland AN68C/2R	NCME	CH43/33F	
1982	PCW 98X	98	Leyland AN68C/2R	NCME	CH43/33F	
1983	ACK 99Y	99	Leyland AN68D/2R	NCME	CH43/33R	
1984	A74 LHG	74	Leyland AN68D/2R	NCME	CH43/33F	
1984	B43 UCK	43	Leyland TRCTL11	Duple	DP47F	
1984	B75 URN	75	Leyland AN68D/2R	NCME	CH43/33F	
1985	C27 ECW	27	Leyland TRCTL11	Duple	C53F	
1985	DBA 227C	89	Leyland PDR1/1	MCCW	O43/33F	Ex LCT
1985	JRH 418E	90	Leyland PDR1/1	Roe	H44/31F	Ex KH
1985	ARH 304K	91	Leyland PDR1A/1	Roe	H43/29F	do
1985	ARH 307K	92	Leyland PDR1A/1	Roe	H43/29F	do
1985	ARH 309K	93	Leyland PDR1A/1	Roe	H43/29F	do
1985	ARH 313K	94	Leyland PDR1A/1	Roe	H43/29F	do

FYLDE BOROUGH TRANSPORT LTD.

YEAR	REG.	FLEET Nos.	CHASSIS Nos	BODY	SEATING	NOTES
1987	D101-4 AFV	101-4	Dodge S56	NCME	B22F	
1987	D105-6 AFV	105-6	Dodge S56	NCME	DP20F	
1987	PRH 243G	127	Leyland PDR1A/1	Roe	H44/31F	Ex KH
1987	TKH 262H	121	Leyland PDR1A/1	Roe	H43/28D	do
1987	TKH 266-7	122-3	Leyland PDR1A/1	Roe	H43/28D	do
1987	TKH 268H	45	Leyland PDR1A/1	Roe	H43/28D	do
1987	TKH 271H	76	Leyland PDR1A/1	Roe	H43/28D	do
1987	TKH 276H	46	Leyland PDR1A/1	Roe	H43/28D	do
1987	WRH 282J	124	Leyland PDR1A/1	Roe	H43/28D	do
1987	WRH 294J	125	Leyland PDR1A/1	Roe	H43/28D	do
1987	WRH 296J	126	Leyland PDR1A/1	Roe	H43/28D	do
1987	ARH 311K	128	Leyland PDR1A/1	Roe	H43/29F	do
1987	SJV 90H	47	Daimler CRG6LX	Roe	H45/29D	Ex GC
1987	UJV 95-6	48-9	Daimler CRG6LX	Roe	H45/29D	do
1987	D912 NBA	107	Dodge S56	NCME	B22F	
1988	E108-14 LCW	108-14	Renault S56	NCME	B25F	
1988	E164 -6 LCW	117-9	Renault S56	NCME	B25F	
1988	F120 UFR	120	Renault S56	NCME	DP27F	
1988	F141-5 UFR	141-5	Renault S56	NCME	B27F	
1988	YNA 398M	31	Leyland PSU3B/4R	Duple	C53F	
1988	YNA 400M	32	Leyland PSU3B/4R	Duple	C53F	
1988	NUT 16W	44	Leyland PSU3F/4R	Duple	C53F	

APPENDIX 2 FLEET LIST SUMMARY

YEAR	REG.	FLEET Nos.	CHASSIS Nos	BODY	SEATING	NOTES
1988	ULS 653T	30	Leyland PSU3E/4R	Duple	C53F	Ex KS
1988	BTB 928	134	Leyland LT7c	Leyland	B34R	Note 2
1988	WRH 291J	133	Leyland PDR1A/1	Roe	H43/28D	Ex KH
1988	WRH 295J	134?	Leyland PDR1A/1	Roe	H43/28D	do
1988	ARH 301K	130	Leyland PDR1A/1	Roe	H43/29F	do
1988	ARH 308K	131	Leyland PDR1A/1	Roe	H43/29F	do
1988	ARH 314K	132	Leyland PDR1A/1	Roe	H43/29F	do
1988	DRH 329L	129	Leyland An68/1R	Roe	H43/29F	do
1989	E385 CNE	115	Renault S56	NCME	B25F	Ex NCME
1989	ONF 659R	161	Leyland An68A/1R	NCME	H43/32F	Ex GMB
1989	ONF 660R	162	Leyland An68A/1R	NCME	H43/32F	do
1989	ONF 664/6/7/9/73R	163-7	Leyland An68A/1R	NCME	H43/32F	do
1989	SRJ 756/7R	168-9	Leyland An68A/1R	NCME	H43/32F	do
1990	MSD 141P	170	Leyland An68A/1R	NCME	H43/34F	Ex CC
1990	TSD 571S	171	Leyland An68A/1R	NCME	H43/34F	do
1991	H1/2/3 FBT	1-3	DAF SB220LC550	Optare	DP48F	
1992	J26 LRN	26	DAFSB3000DKV601	Van Hool	C51FT	
1992	TKH 261H	47	Leyland PDR1A/1R	Roe	H43/28D	Ex KH
1992	TKU 462/5/6/9K		Leyland PDR2/1	-	-	Ex KH Chassis only
1992	ARH 292K	92	Leyland PDR1A/1R	Roe	H43/29F	Ex KH
1992	DRH 327/30L	92,88	Leyland An68/1R	Roe	H43/29F	do
1992	ARH 306K	93	Leyland PDR1A/1R	Roe	H43/29F	do
1992	DRH 331L		Leyland An68A/1R	Roe	H43/29R	do
1992	NAT 339M	87	Leyland An68A/1R	Roe	H43/29F	do
1993	G812/3 RNC	24,25	Leyland TR2R62	Plaxton	C51F	Ex Sh
1994	URN 322-7V	322-7	Leyland An68A/2R	East Lancs	H50/36F	Ex Bl
1994	B364 UBV	47	Leyland An68D/2R	East Lancs	CH45/29F	do
1995	URN 328-30	328-30	Leyland An68A/2R	East Lancs	H50/36F	do
1995	G101-2 NBV	8,9	DAFSB220LC550	Optare	DP46F	do
1995	F699/700/703ENE	21-23	Leyland TRCL10/	Plaxton	C53F	Ex TT
1996	N201-8 LCK	201-8	Optare Excel	Optare	B36F	
1996	AHG 331/4V	331/4	Leyland An68A/2R	East Lancs	H50/36R	Ex Bl
1996	UWW 5/11/15X	365-7	Leyland ONLXB/1R	Roe	H47/29F	do

Notes :-
1. NCME frames finished by Willowbrook and supplied by Yeates. See text for further details.
2. Original Lytham St. Annes vehicle re purchased by Fylde from preservationist. See text for further details.
Ex ES indicates ex Ellen Smith, Rochdale
Ex CrMS indicates ex Crosville Motor Services Ltd.
Ex LCT indicates Ex Lancaster City Transport
Ex WCT indicates ex Warrington Corporation Transport
Ex Mside indicates ex Merseyside PTE
Ex RMS indicates ex Ribble Motor Services
Ex KH incicates ex Kingston upon Hull City Transport
Ex NCME indicates ex Northern Counties Motor and Engineering Co. Ltd.
Ex GC indicates ex Grimsby Cleethorpes Transport.
Ex KS indicates ex Kelvin Scottish
Ex Sh. indicates ex Shearings
Ex Ex Bl indicates ex Blackpool Corporation Transport or Blackpool Transport Services Ltd.
Ex TT indicates ex Timeline Travel

Fleet Numbers. The fleet numbers indicated are those allocated when the vehicle was purchased. Many vehicles were renumbered during their time with Fylde and details of the renumbering are given in the PSV Circle Publication PC25 'Fylde Transport Ltd. and its Successors'

APPENDIX 3

SCHEDULE OF BUS SERVICES AS AT MARCH 1928

Route	Details	Joint Operator/Notes
1a	St. Annes Centre - Albert Road.	
2	St. Annes Centre - Leach Lane	
3	St. Annes Centre - Old Links	
4	St.Annes - Lytham - Green Drive	
5	Lytham Square -, Meadows Lane	

APPENDIX 4

SCHEDULE OF BUS SERVICES AS AT 29th October 1973

On 29th October 1973 a 'Commemorative Time & Fare Table' booklet was issued to mark the forthcomming demise of Lytham St.Annes Corporation Transport on 31st March 1974 as part of Local Government reorganisation. The following services were listed in the booklet :-

Route	Details	Joint Operator/Notes
1	Squires Gate (Halfway house) - Lytham Square via St.Annes	Most Journeys commenced St.Annes Square, Commonside, South Park Square. No Evening or Sun. Service
2	St.Annes Square - Smithy Lane	No evening or Sun. Service
3	Spring Gardens - Lytham Square via St.Annes Square.	Evenings & Sun. Spring Gardens - St. Annes
4	St.Annes Square - Lytham Green Drive via Heyhouses Lane, Ansdell, Clifton Drive	
11	Blackpool Talbot Road - Lytham Meadow Lane via St.Annes Road, St.Annes Square, Church Road	Joint with Blackpool Transport No Sun. service - see 31
11A	Blackpool Talbot Road - Lytham Meadow Lane via Central Drive, Lytham Road, St.Annes Square	Joint with Blackpool Transport Occasional journeys only
11C	Blackpool Talbot Road - St.Annes Square via Queensway	Operated by Blackpool Transport Daily
31	Blackpool Talbot Road - Lytham Saltcoats Road via St.Annes Road, St.Annes Square, Church Road	Joint with Blackpool Transport Suns.only
31A	Blackpool Talbot Road - Lytham Salcoats Road via via Central Drive, Lytham Road, St.Annes Square	Joint with Blackpool Transport Daily

Schools Services

S1	Spring Gardens - Queen Mary School	
S2	Clifton Drive North - St.Thomas's School	
S3	Spring Gardens - St.Bede's School, Lytham	
S4	Heeley Road, East - Ansdell School	
S5	Spring Gardens - St.Thomas's School	
S6	Spring Gardens - Ansdell Couny School	
B	Starr Gate - Common Edge School	Operated on behalf of Blackpool Corporation Transport.

Note.
The Sunday timings for service 11C are shown ex Talbot Road Bus Station as :-
0940 and every 24 minutes until 2140, 2208, 2235.
This must have made it very difficult for intending passengers to to determine departure times between 0940 and 2140.

APPENDIX 5

SCHEDULE OF BUS SERVICES AS AT 26th October 1986

Route	Details	Notes
2	Blackpool Talbot Rd.Bus Sta. - Poulton via Newton Drive	Daily
3	Blackpool Gynn Sq. - Mereside via Talbot Rd. Park Rd. Oxford Sq.	Daily
4	St.Annes Squre - Lytham Square via Commonside	M-S Roamer Service
7	Blackpool Talbot Rd. Bus Sta. - Bispham Hotel via Devonshire Rd. return via Warbreck Drive	Evenings Operated on behalf of LCC
7A	Blackpool Talbot Rd. Bus Sta. - Bispham Hotel via Warbreck Drive return vis Devonshire Rd	do.
8	Blackpool Talbot Rd. Bus Sta. - Whiteholme via Bispham Hotel, Technical College	M-S Operated on behalf of LCC
8A	St.Annes Square - St.Annes Hospice	M-S Operated on behalf of LCC
11	Talbot Rd. Bus Sta. - Lytham Saltcoates Rd. via St.Annes Sq. Church Rd. Lytham Sq.	Daily
11A	Talbot Rd. Bus Sta. - Lytham Saltcoates Rd. via St. Annes Sq., Clifton Drive, Lytham Sq.	Daily
11C	Talbot Road Bus Sta. - St. Annes Square via Common Edge Rd.	Daily
13	Talbot Rd. Bus Sta. - Bispham Hotel via Dumfries Close	Tuesdays and Fridays only Operated on behalf of LCC.
15	Talbot Rd. Bus Sta. - Staining via Newton Drive	Daily. Su. operation on Behalf of LCC
21	Talbot Rd. Bus Sta. - Lytham Square via Chapel Street, St. Annes Sq. Fairhaven Hotel	Limited Stop M-S
31	Talbot Rd. Bus Sta. - Lytham Sq. via Manchester Sq. St.Annes Sq. Commonside	Limited Stop M-S
23A	Blackpool South Pier - Mereside via Lindale Gardens, Welcome Inn.	Evenings and Sundays Operation on behalf of LCC
190/191	Blackpool Talbot Rd. Bus Sta. - Gt. Eccleston via Poulton	M-S
192	Blackpool Talbot Rd. Bus Sta. - Kirkham via Poulton, Elswick, Wesham	Daily
193 via	Wesham - Spring Gardens Kirkham, Freckleton, Lytham, St. Annes.	Daily Some journeys on services 190-193 operated on behalf of LCC On Su. some 193 journeys operated to/from Talbot Rd.
780	Fleetwood - Poulton Railway Station behalf of LCC	M-F one journey in each direction via Thornton

School Services

Route	Details	Notes
G3	Talbot Rd. Bus Sta. - King Edward/Queen Mary Sch.	Schooldays
G5	Lytham Saltcoates Rd. - Elmslie/St.Mary's/ Collegiate High School	Schooldays
G6	Lytham Square - Arnold School	Schooldays
G7	Arnold School - Lytham Square.	Schooldays except Fridays

G8	Fleetwood - Elmslie School via Poulton	Schooldays
G9	Preston - Elmslie School via Kirkham	Schooldays
S1	Queen Mary School - Spring Gardens	Schooldays
S2	St.Annes - St.Thomas'/LythamSt.Annes HighSchool	Schooldays
S3	Blackpool Arnold Ave. - Lytham St.Annes High School St. Bedes School	Schooldays
S4	St.Annes - Lytham St.Annes High School /St.Bedes	Schooldays
S5	Spring Gardens - St.Thomas' School	Schooldays
S7	Cleveleys Bus Sta. - Baines School, Poulton	Schooldays Operated on behalf of LCC
S10	Our Lady School - Manchester Square, Blackpool	Schooldays Operated on behalf of LCC
S12	Lytham St.Annes High School - St.Annes Clifton Dr.N.	Scholdays
S15	Lytham St.Annes High School - Spring Gardens	Schooldays
S22	Carlton Crossing - Hodgson High School	Schooldays Operated on behalf of LCC
S25	Lytham St.Annes RC School - Spring gardens	Schooldays
S26	Leyland Cross - King Edward/Queen Mary School	Schooldays Operated onbehalf of LCC

Other Special Services

H1	Wrea Green - Blackpool Hospitals	Wed/Thu. No fare charged. Service provided by Fylde Borough Council
W16	Cleveleys Bus Sta. - Norcross (DHSS)	M-F Operated on behalf of LCC
W80	Poulton Aldon Rd. - Blackpool Talbot Rd. Bus Sta.	M-F Single journey on behalf of LCC.

APPENDIX 6

SCHEDULE OF BUS SERVICES AS AT 1994

Route	Details	Joint Operator/Notes
1	St Annes Square - Uncle Tom's Cabin via Pontins, Blackpool Promenade	Summer Only
11	Cleveleys - Lytham via Bispham, Blackpool, St Annes Road, St Annes Church Road	Evenings & Suns. Blackpool - Lytham only
11A	Cleveleys - Lytham via Bispham, Blackpool, Lytham Road, St Annes Clifton Drive	Evenings & Suns. Blackpool - Lytham, Kirham & Wesham
11C	Blackpool - St Annes Square via Queensway	
33	Mereside - Cleveleys via Park Road, Blackpool, Bispham, Norbreck	No evening or Sun. service
44/44A	Mereside - Cleveleys via Marton Mere, Blackpool	No evening or Sun. service
77	St Annes Roamer	No evening or Sun. service
193	St Annes Square - Kirkham and Wesham via Clifton Drive, Lytham, Warton, Freckleton	No evening or Sun. service See 11A
333	Marton Mere - Fleetwood via Blackpool, Cleveleys.	Evenings and Suns. only
444	Mereside - Cleveleys via Blackpool	Evenings and Suns. only
154/158	Blackpool - Preston via Marton, Kirkham	Evenings and Suns. only
NB	Services 154, 158, 333 and 444 were operated on behalf of Lancashire County Council	

Acknowledgements

The author and publisher acknowledge with gratitude the help of many organisations and individuals in the preparation of this book. John Nye, a former General Manager, has read the text and made useful comment and also provided some wonderful photographs from his collection. Mike Sagrott, former Engineering Director, has provided useful information and photographs. The assistance of the Lytham Heritage Group, particularly that of Steve Williams, deputy chairman, and also the ladies in the archive room at the library , has been very much appreciated. Their assistance included the provision of some excellent photographs. Peter Jaques found the splendid coloured postcard of trams at the Gynn terminus whilst Ian Stewart allowed us to use his magnificent drawing of one of Lytham's famous open-sided double-deck trams.

Reference has been made to various periodicals including Buses Magazine, Classic Bus, Commercial Motor and Tramway & Railway World. Reference has also been made to 'The Tramways of Lytham St Annes' by P H Abell, J A Garnham and I Mc.Loughlin, published by The Oakwood Press and to 'Looking back at Blue Buses' by Philip Higgs published by Lancastria Transport Publications. As ever, the publications of the Omnibus Society and the PSV Circle have provided invaluable information, particularly the PSV Circle publication PC25 - 'A Fleet History of Fylde Transport Limited and its predecessors.

The author is especially grateful to John and Mark Senior together with Bob Rowe at Venture Publications and also to Scott Halliwell for the production of the map. David and Mary Shaw have, as ever, meticulously checked the proofs but any errors are mine and not theirs.

Acknowledgement is made to the many photographers without whose help this book would not have materialised. These include Roy Marshall, Bob Downham, Mark Bailey, Ken Swallow, Michael Morton, Michael Sagrott , the Leyland BCVM Collection and the Senior Transport archive. Steve Palmer also made available photographs from his extensive collection. Where the source of the photograph is known, acknowledgement has been made on the individual photograph using the key below. As is usually the case, some photographs have no indication as to their origin and these are credited to the persons who have loaned them from their collections. If therefore we have wrongly attributed any images, or missed out any contributors, we apologise in advance.

Harry Postlethwaite,
Blackpool,
August 2009.

Photographic Key

MB	Mark Bailey	RM	Roy Marshall
KS	Ken Swallow	BD	Bob Downham
MM	Michael Morton	MS	Mike Sagrott
STA	Senior Transport Archive	SPC	Steve Palmer Collection
LHG	Lytham Heritage Group	JNC	John Nye Collection
HP	Author	HPC	Author's Collection
Kithead	The Kithead Archive	LM	Leyland Motors